Contents

Introduction

"Should I kill myself or have a cup of coffee?"

It's a striking question—at once absurd and profound—and a fitting way to open a meditation on the tensions of existence. Attributed to Albert Camus, the line encapsulates the essential confrontation at the heart of existential philosophy: the stark juxtaposition of annihilation and routine. It invites us to consider not just whether life is worth living, but whether the smallest acts of participation in life—like making a cup of coffee—can themselves be meaning enough.

This book is born from that question.

Existentialism, particularly in its 20th-century articulation, challenges us to take radical responsibility for our freedom, even in a universe that appears cold and indifferent. It is a philosophy not of despair, but of confrontation. At its core lies the concept of the **absurd**—the tension between our longing for meaning and the universe's silence in return. In that confrontation, we do not retreat; we respond.

The cup of coffee, then, is not incidental. It becomes emblematic—a symbol of presence, of choosing to engage, to continue, to create rhythm and ritual in the face of uncertainty. It is a modest but resolute affirmation that life, however fragmented or uncertain, still invites participation.

To choose the coffee is to choose life.

It is in the act of choosing—of continuing despite the void, of acting despite the uncertainty—that existential philosophy finds its power. It offers no easy answers, no comforting illusions. Instead, it challenges us to cultivate meaning through engagement, to define ourselves through action, and to derive purpose not from what the world gives, but from how we respond to it.

As I reflect on my own motivation to write this book, I do so not merely as a thinker or writer, but as a human being who has wrestled with the contradictions of life—its darkness and its beauty, its alienation and its intimacy. I bring to this work not a set of pre-scriptions, but a deep empathy for those navigating the gray waters of hopelessness, existential fatigue, and quiet despair. I have lived long enough—and studied widely enough—to know that the choice to live is not always easy, and that even mundane acts can carry the weight of quiet heroism.

This book is not a manual for happiness, nor a blueprint for salvation. Rather, it is an invitation—to reflect, to feel, to question, and perhaps to see your morning coffee not as an empty ritual, but as an act of rebellion, a declaration of intent, and a gentle yet firm "yes" to life.

In the pages that follow, I will explore how existentialism and absurdism provide not just a framework for thought, but a posture for living. I will argue that in the face of chaos, we must seek not control, but **virtue**—and that in embracing our freedom, we embrace the very thing that makes life worth the struggle.

This is a book about the courage to continue.

This is a book about choosing coffee.

The final monologue of Danny Boyle's 1996 film "Trainspotting" encapsulates our journey ahead:

Now I'm cleaning up and I'm moving on, going straight and choosing life. I'm looking forward to it already. I'm gonna be just like you. The job, the family, the fucking big television. The washing machine, the car, the compact disc and electric tin opener, good health, low cholesterol, dental insurance, mortgage, starter home, leisure wear, luggage, three piece suite, DIY, game shows, junk food, children, walks in the park, nine to five, good at golf, washing the car, choice of sweaters, family Christmas, indexed pension, tax exemption, clearing gutters, getting by, looking ahead, the day you die.

There's a little sarcasm in this speech, but the point is that he recognizes the absurdity of our existence and that there seems to be little-to-no point in anything, but he's going to press on regardless. And so should we.

Chapter 1
The Nihilism Deluge

"If we believe in nothing, if nothing has any meaning and if we can affirm no values whatsoever, then everything is possible and nothing has any importance."
Albert Camus

Nihilism has deeply permeated our culture and society in the 21st century. This chapter seeks to examine the origins and expressions of nihilism, delving into its influence on philosophy, contemporary culture, and individuals.

In order to grasp the impact of nihilism, it is imperative to first comprehend its fundamental nature. It's not just an abstract philosophical idea; nihilism is a complete way of looking at things that rejects any meaning or worth in existence. This pessimistic viewpoint has significant consequences for how we might perceive the world around us, if we were to associate with it that is.

Nihilism questions the fundamental principles of conventional belief systems, asserting that life does not possess inherent meaning or purpose. The notion that there exists no absolute truth or inherent worthiness compels us to confront the notion of potentially forging our own sense of purpose, a disconcerting prospect for many of us.

Exploring the historical origins of nihilism uncovers its development as a reaction to changes in society and culture. Friedrich Nietzsche and Arthur Schopenhauer, philosophers of the 19th century, established the foundation for nihilistic ideology by questioning conventional concepts of morality and metaphysics. Modern nihilism is no different as evidenced by this passage from Chuck Palahniuk's *Fight Club:*

"I see in the fight club the strongest and smartest men who've ever lived. I see all this potential and I see squandering. God damn it, an entire generation pumping gas, waiting tables, slaves with white collars, advertising has us chasing cars and clothes, working jobs we hate so we can buy shit we don't need. We're the middle children of the history man, no purpose or place, we have no Great war, no Great depression, our great war is a spiritual war, our great depression is our lives, we've been all raised by television to believe that one day we'd all be millionaires and movie gods and rock stars, but we won't and we're slowly learning that fact. and we're very very pissed off."

One component of nihilism, the one which challenges accepted beliefs and norms, tends to be popular with people who are new to philosophy and played an integral role in its rise from the late 19th century to the mid 20th century. To deal with the emptiness that nihilism caused over that period, philosophers thought about what would happen if we truly believed the universe didn't have any inclination to provide us with meaning or purpose while we're here. This, as we know, led to the rise of existentialist philosophy.

Nihilistic philosophical movements questioned the very nature of human life, forcing us to face emptiness and find meaning in a universe that 1) seems to have no purpose and 2) has no interest in what we do while we're living in it.

As we transition from theoretical concepts to actual circumstances (this is not an introduction on nihilism afterall), the impact of nihilism on contemporary culture becomes apparent. I mean, we see it everywhere. Artistic expressions, ranging from movies to music, often incorporate nihilistic themes, which serve as a reflection of a society that is struggling with the lack of a universally accepted purpose or meaning.

Literary works, spanning from timeless masterpieces to modern novels, frequently engage with nihilistic themes. Authors use their stories to look into the complicated parts of being human in a world where *meaning* needs to be carefully constructed since it's anything but universal. Nihilism in literature transcends any particular genre or style, instead permeating as an all-encompassing undertone that influences the development of characters and narratives. Literature acts as a reflective tool, showcasing the nihilistic trends of the present era, ranging from bleak depictions of a purposeless future to deep introspections on personal meaning-making. Read any Cormac Mc-Carthy novel or any of the hundreds of novels he's inspired.

Nihilistic artists use art, whether it's making things or putting on performances, to show how they feel and what they think of the world they're inhabiting. The lack of predetermined meaning allows for a deep exploration of what it means to be human. Nihilistic art subverts traditional norms and expectations, prompting us to confront the unease of a world devoid of inherent purpose. It challenges conventional interpretations through abstract paintings and performances that provoke introspection, pushing the boundaries of artistic expression.

The prevalence of nihilistic themes in both art and pop culture is not solely a manifestation of individual artists' viewpoints. Instead, it reflects the wider societal recognition of a world that frequently seems to lack any objective meaning or inherent worth. Let's take a look at a few examples in film, television, music, literature, and the visual arts.

"Fight Club," a film helmed by David Fincher based on the book by Chuck Palahniuk, incorporates nihilistic themes as it critiques consumer culture and explores existential angst. The main character, whose name is not given, feels like he has no purpose in life until he meets Tyler Durden, a reflection of his shadow self. The act of embracing this version of himself is what comprises the first few acts of the story and the film is mostly about nihilistic rejection of social norms, consumerism, and the search for one's own identity.

The Coen Brothers' film adaptation of Cormac McCarthy's novel "No Country for Old Men" explores nihilism by focusing on the character of Anton Chigurh. His unwavering determination and ruthless aggression epitomize a nihilistic perspective, mirroring a disorderly cosmos lacking in ethical certainties or repercussions.

"The Sopranos," the highly praised television series of the late 1990s, combines elements of organized crime drama with deep existential exploration. Tony Soprano, the morally ambiguous main character, struggles with the lack of purpose in his own life, reflecting the nihilistic undertones of a world where power and violence frequently overshadow significance and ethics.

"BoJack Horseman" is an animated series that explores the life of a former successful actor. The show tackles nihilistic concepts like existential hopelessness, substance dependence, and the quest for purpose. The protagonist's voyage transforms into a poignant examination of the emptiness that accompanies fame and achievement.

Bret Easton Ellis novel "American Psycho" functions as a harsh criticism of consumerism and the emptiness of the American Dream. Patrick Bateman, the main character, exemplifies nihilistic inclinations through his fixation on materialism, lack of moral principles, and the dehumanizing consequences of societal norms.

Cormac McCarthy portrays a desolate and nihilistic world in his dystopian novel "The Road". The expedition undertaken by a paternal figure and his offspring across a barren terrain functions as an investigation into the philosophical concept of nihilism when confronted with a profound sense of existential emptiness.

"Smells Like Teen Spirit," Nirvana's grunge masterpiece, serves as the anthem of a generation, effectively encapsulating the feelings of disillusionment and apathy prevalent during the 1990s. Kurt Cobain captures the nihilistic essence that defies societal norms and conventional ideas of achievement with lyrics such as "Here we are now, entertain us."

Radiohead's album "OK Computer" explores profound subjects such as the feeling of being isolated from technology, the disconnection from society, and the unease that comes with living in the modern world. The band's examination of a dystopian future reflects nihilistic anxieties regarding the gradual disappearance of significance in a society controlled by technology.

The military shooter video game "Spec Ops: The Line" challenges conventional gaming narratives by embracing the horrific psychological consequences of warfare. The game presents players with moral dilemmas and shows them the outcomes of their decisions, thereby questioning the notion of heroism and highlighting nihilistic themes.

The "Dark Souls" series, a third-person RPG fantasy video game series, is renowned for its demanding gameplay and enigmatic storyline, which includes a number of nihilistic themes. The relentless nature of the game world, combined with themes of existential strife and unavoidable deterioration, corresponds to the nihilistic concept of a brutal and apathetic universe.

In the visual arts arena, Banksy, an enigmatic street artist, frequently integrates nihilistic motifs into his politically provocative artworks. Artworks such as "There Is Always Hope" (2003), which depicts a balloon drifting away, raise doubts about the effectiveness of hope in a world characterized by social, political, and environmental crises.

Another artist named Yayoi Kusama produced such masterpieces as the "Infinity Mirrored Room—The Souls of Millions of Light Years Away" (2013) which elicit a feeling of existential emptiness on a cosmic scale. The recurrence and enormity in her work reflect the existential insignificance experienced when confronted with an infinite and apathetic universe.

The creators of and behind the above mentioned works were without doubt influenced by nihilistic ideas and tendencies and understanding the origin of works of art like this is actually beneficial to us, the consumers, in that we witness and/or experience another person's view of their own abyss.

Nihilism, if embraced, shapes more than just our beliefs; it shapes the *way* we think and *what* we believe in general. Loss of a shared understanding over time can lead to the breakdown of social cohesion, as groups struggle to find common points of view in a world where individual interpretations are the norm. Imagine yourself on a boat and every person on board wanted the boat to go somewhere other than where you wanted it to go.

And because of this, nihilism serves as a disruptive influence in society, questioning and challenging established norms and institutions, not all of which are bad and need to be torn down. The absence of a commonly held moral or existential framework can result in a void, causing us (and our communities) to feel lost amidst a multitude of conflicting ideologies and subjective truths.

The influence of nihilism on society is not consistently detrimental, however. Advocates claim that it promotes individual liberty and independence by freeing us from predetermined interpretations and enabling a more flexible and evolving social framework. There are actually a number of books that encourage readers to embrace passive nihilism as a way of life.

In the midst of prevailing nihilistic trends, we are faced with the challenge of navigating the intricacies of a seemingly purposeless world. Learning how to cope is an important way to fight the nihilistic trend we're seeing, and a lot of psychologists and counselors are looking for training and support to better provide them to their clients.

Existentialism emerges as a contrasting response to nihilism, highlighting the significance of individual autonomy and the formation of subjective significance. This shift prompts us to seek meaning through our own endeavors, thereby confronting the existential emptiness of nihilism. Existentialism proposes that we possess the agency to determine our own fate, serving as a mechanism for coping. By accepting the concept that existence comes before essence, we can find significance in our experiences, relationships, and achievements.

The adoption and understanding of existentialism as a coping mechanism does not entail a rejection of nihilistic realities, but rather a proactive and deliberate response to them (i.e. choosing coffee over the alternative every morning). It signifies a deliberate attempt to confront the emptiness caused by nihilism and construct a purposeful existence in its absence. *Even though there doesn't seem to be a reason why I exist, I exist nonetheless and should perhaps get to work thinking about why.*

The emergence of existentialism as a response to nihilism is not simply a philosophical fad, but rather a crucial cultural and psychological requirement. Amidst the presence of nihilistic forces that pose a risk of overwhelming us with existential hopelessness, existentialism offers a life-saving vessel—a method for successfully navigating the turbulent depths of purposelessness.

When confronted with an option of giving one's life over to passive nihilism, we should remember that we have the option to find purpose in personal relationships, creative pursuits, or societal contributions.

The quest for meaning is a distinct experience for all of us, highlighting the inherent uniqueness in a world that lacks a universal objective.

To discover significance in a nihilistic world, we must deviate from conventional outlets of meaning. It requires a willingness to investigate non-traditional approaches and a readiness to acknowledge that meaning is a subjective creation, influenced by personal experiences and interpretations.

Chapter 2
What Do We Really Need?

I kept landing on Maslow's Hierarchy of Needs for one reason or another as I conducted research for this book. I think it may provide value to use his model to answer the question: *What do we really need?*

The structured model known as Maslow's Hierarchy of Needs illustrates human motivations arranged in a pyramid-like structure. The hierarchy is based on fundamental physiological needs, which are then followed by safety, social belongingness, esteem, and ultimately culminate in self-actualization. The hierarchical arrangement suggests that we must fulfill their lower-level needs before we can move on to higher-level ones, highlighting the dynamic nature of human motivation.

Maslow distinguishes between deficiency needs, which stem from a deprivation and motivate us to pursue fulfillment, and growth needs, which signify a yearning for self-improvement and transcendence. Self-actualization is found in the category of growth needs. It involves striving to reach one's highest potential and experiencing a deep sense of satisfaction.

Self-actualization, as defined by Maslow, refers to the achievement of one's full potential, self-awareness, and the active pursuit of personal growth and peak experiences. It includes a collection of attributes such as independence, genuineness, innovation, meaning, and a continuous pursuit of self-improvement. As I explore the complexities of self-actualization, I am impressed by its multifaceted nature, which encompasses a comprehensive approach to human well-being.

Self-actualization, which represents the highest level of human potential, is only attained by a minority of individuals, according to Maslow's proposition. The paradox lies in the infrequency of achieving self-actualization despite its widespread existence as a fundamental human requirement. This puzzle encourages a more thorough investigation into the elements that either facilitate or impede the process of achieving one's full potential.

Autonomy is a key trait of self-actualization, representing the ability to make independent decisions and behave in accordance with one's personal beliefs. Authenticity is a trait that entails a sincere and genuine manifestation of one's true self. Those of us who are striving for self-actualization demonstrate a deep sense of genuineness, fully accepting and embodying our authentic selves without conforming to external pressures or societal norms.

Creativity is a significant aspect of self-actualization. The process of generating, whether through artistic endeavors, inventive thinking, or resolving challenges, serves as a vehicle for self-expression and a route to unlocking undiscovered capabilities. The investigation of creativity within the context of self-actualization reveals its dual nature as both a process and a result—a voyage and an endpoint.

Self-actualized individuals exhibit a profound sense of purpose and significance in their lives. The endeavor to achieve a noble purpose or an elevated objective becomes a compelling motivation. As I reflect on the relationship between purpose and self-actualization, I am inclined to believe that a meaningful life is closely tied to the fulfillment of one's individual capabilities.

The pursuit of self-actualization is characterized by a dedication to ongoing personal development. Self-actualized individuals actively pursue continuous learning throughout their lives, consistently striving to broaden their perspectives and enhance their comprehension of both themselves and the world. Maslow also presents the notion of peak experiences, which are significant instances of transcendence and heightened consciousness that occur intermittently in the lives of individuals who are striving for self-actualization.

Peak experiences, as defined by Maslow, refer to highly intense instances of happiness, satisfaction, and heightened consciousness. These experiences, whether they occur unexpectedly or are intentionally pursued, act as triggers for individual development and the realization of one's full potential. As I examine the significance of peak experiences, I am impressed by their profound ability to influence an individual's perception of themselves and the world. Over the last few years I've tried to create opportunities for peak experiences in both ultramarathons and Spartan Races.

Self-actualized individuals derive motivation from their most significant and fulfilling moments, incorporating the knowledge gained and utilizing it as a source of innovation, meaning, and ongoing development. The repetition of peak experiences enhances an elevated level of awareness, promoting a profound bond with the inherent worth of life and the quest for self-actualization. How you feel after completing something incredibly difficult is what is meant by "elevated level of awareness" here.

The path to self-actualization is not without obstacles. Cultural and societal norms, expectations, and constraints can hinder the expression of individuality and suppress the pursuit of genuine self-hood. As I strive to achieve personal growth, I struggle with the conflict between societal norms and the need to live authentically. I have a doctorate in educational leadership, but I would rather spend time in classrooms with students than put out fires in an administrative role. I learned this a few years after earning my PhD and am now seen as someone who is underachieving because my goals have shifted.

Psychological obstacles, such as the apprehension of failure and the apprehension of success, can hinder the progress towards achieving your full potential. The phobia of failure, which originates from the underlying fear of not meeting expectations (either your own or someone else's for you), has the potential to immobilize us, impeding our inclination to take chances and strive for our ambitions. On the other hand, the fear of success, which is often disregarded, stems from the apprehension related to the obligations and transformations that success might entail. Both fears, despite appearing to be contradictory, are rooted in a shared apprehension of the unfamiliar and have the potential to hinder the realization of one's genuine capabilities.

The constant pursuit of approval from others, known as external validation, presents a major barrier to achieving self-actualization. The longing for social acceptance can compel individuals to adhere to societal conventions, relinquishing their true selves in the process. The conflict between the desire for validation and the longing for authentic self-expression presents a division that poses a challenge to an individual's pursuit of self-fulfillment. This is a problem and theme I explore almost weekly across all of my social accounts.

Lack of self-awareness serves as a primary obstacle to achieving self-actualization. Individuals who lack a profound comprehension of their values, strengths, and aspirations may find themselves adrift, lacking a sense of connection to their true selves. The process of

self-discovery, which is crucial for achieving self-actualization, necessitates a dedicated practice of self-reflection and a resolute readiness to
confront the intricacies of one's own identity.

The process of achieving self-actualization begins by developing
self-awareness. This entails a purposeful examination of an individual's principles, interests, capabilities, and constraints. Practices such
as mindfulness, introspection, and reflective journaling are utilized as
means to uncover and understand one's true identity, enabling individuals to harmonize their lives with their genuine selves.

Self-actualization necessitates a readiness to accept vulnerability,
displaying the bravery to be transparent and genuine even in the face
of potential criticism or disappointment. Paradoxically, this vulnerability transforms into a reservoir of power. When combined with
resilience, which is the capacity to recover quickly from difficulties
and obstacles, it creates a powerful interaction that drives individuals
towards achieving their full potential.

A growth mindset, based on the conviction that skills and intellect
can be enhanced through commitment and effort, is crucial in the
quest for self-fulfillment. Adopting challenges as chances for personal
development, fostering a passion for acquiring knowledge, and perceiving obstacles as progress markers rather than barriers all contribute
to the resilience necessary for the journey.

Positive psychology, a discipline that examines the positive aspects
and qualities that empower individuals to flourish, intersects with
Maslow's Hierarchy of Needs, specifically in relation to self-actualization. Positive psychologists, drawing inspiration from Maslow's
focus on human potential, investigate ways to improve well-being,
cultivate positive emotions, and create an environment that supports
self-fulfillment.

The notion of flourishing, which is fundamental to positive psychology, corresponds with the apex of Maslow's Hierarchy. Flourishing extends beyond mere happiness and involves a comprehensive state of well-being that includes the development of personal strengths, positive connections with others, a sense of purpose, and a profound feeling of satisfaction. While traversing this intersection, I am intrigued by the mutual objective of both frameworks—to unravel the enigmas surrounding human flourishing and contentment.

The pursuit of personal self-fulfillment, contrary to being an isolated endeavor, has the capacity to generate a domino effect in society. Individuals who have achieved self-actualization, by demonstrating qualities such as authenticity, creativity, and purpose, make positive contributions to their communities. The shared endeavor of achieving self-actualization serves as a catalyst for the advancement of society, by questioning established norms and creating a nurturing environment that promotes personal development.

Education plays a vital role in enabling individuals to achieve self-actualization. Education systems that prioritize the comprehensive development of individuals, nurture creativity, and promote critical thinking create an ideal environment for the growth and realization of one's full potential. Incorporating Maslow's principles into educational practices has the potential to mold future generations who are adept at navigating the intricacies of the human experience.

To summarize, the examination of self-actualization within Maslow's Hierarchy of Needs reveals a deep and meaningful process characterized by self-reflection, ingenuity, and a relentless commitment to individual development. As I contemplate the intricacies involved in reaching the highest point of human capability, I am reminded of the contradictory essence of self-actualization. It is both something that is common to all and yet difficult to achieve, a goal that is shared by many but pursued in a distinctively personal manner.

The insights derived from Maslow's framework transcend mere theoretical constructs; they function as a roadmap for individuals endeavoring to comprehend the complexities of their own being. The journey of self-actualization involves exploring one's own characteristics and overcoming obstacles along the way, resulting in a continuous and evolving dialogue with oneself.

As we all work together to reach the highest levels of human capability, the importance of self-actualization becomes clear as a reminder to be true to ourselves, embrace our creativity, and find our purpose. The investigation of this highest point in Maslow's Hierarchy compels individuals to embark on a profound and life-changing journey—one that surpasses the boundaries of what is familiar and encourages the development of untapped human capabilities.

Chapter 3
The Problems with the Self-Help Industry

The self-help industry, a dominant force in the contemporary realm of personal growth, offers us the prospect of empowerment, metamorphosis, and the means to unlock our utmost capabilities. The industry saturates society with a plethora of books (this book may actually end up in that category), seminars, podcasts, and apps, providing an apparently limitless range of tools for self-improvement. Nevertheless, beneath the polished facade of this lucrative industry, there are numerous unintended issues and outcomes that warrant careful scrutiny. This chapter explores the uncharted territory of the self-help industry, examining the intricacies and difficulties it presents in people's lives.

The self-help industry encompasses a wide range of products and services designed to aid individuals in attaining personal development, accomplishment, and overall welfare. The industry serves a wide range of individuals seeking guidance in various areas such as career progression, relationship enhancement, mental well-being, and spiritual enlightenment, through motivational speakers and mindfulness apps.

An inherent issue within the self-help industry is the perpetuation of the false belief in immediate solutions and rapid personal growth. Numerous self-improvement products make claims of swift outcomes, targeting the inclination for immediate transformation in a time characterized by impatience and a craving for instant satisfaction. In my zeal to "lessen the suffering" of people I've mistakenly contributed to this problem.

Many people, enticed by the promise of quick and easy progress, frequently face impractical anticipations. The disparity between these expectations and the gradual pace of authentic personal growth can result in disillusionment, exasperation, and a feeling of inadequacy. The industry itself, intended to promote growth, may unintentionally contribute to a cycle of disappointment.

Although the self-help industry claims to have a noble objective of assisting us in our pursuit of personal growth, it is still susceptible to the impact of commercial interests. The pursuit of profit can sometimes overshadow the sincere desire to help, resulting in the development of products and services that prioritize market dominance rather than making a meaningful impact.

The commercialization of personal growth can unintentionally sustain consumerism and materialism. We may be under the impression that acquiring the most recent self-help publication, participating in a costly seminar, or enrolling in high-end coaching programs is the ultimate path to self-fulfillment. The focus on the consumer can divert attention from the more profound elements of personal development.

An ongoing problem in the self-help industry is the inclination to embrace a universal approach that is applicable to everyone. Several widely embraced self-help strategies, often based on anecdotal triumphs, may fail to acknowledge the intricate and varied experiences of individuals. This process of homogenization fails to acknowledge the distinctiveness of individual experiences, which may result in isolating those whose paths deviate from the predetermined pattern. I realized this early on when I began teaching stoicism online. I came to terms with it not being for everyone fairly quickly.

The field of human psychology is characterized by its multifaceted nature, as individuals navigate a complex interplay of emotions, experiences, and circumstances. The self-help industry's tendency to favor simplified solutions may overlook the complexities of the human psyche, potentially resulting in incomplete or misguided interventions.

An omnipresent problem within the self-help industry is the overemphasis on positivity as a panacea for the difficulties encountered in life. Although developing a positive mindset is unquestionably beneficial, the burden of upholding a constant state of positivity can have negative consequences. People may experience a strong urge to hide their true emotions, resulting in a false display of happiness that masks underlying difficulties.

The concept of toxic positivity refers to the tendency to excessively focus on positive emotions and deny or suppress negative emotions. This can be detrimental to one's emotional well-being and hinder personal growth and self-awareness.

The phenomenon of toxic positivity can emerge from the cult of positivity, which entails an unwavering commitment to maintaining a positive mindset, even when confronted with challenging circumstances. The refusal to acknowledge and confront one's emotions, driven by societal pressures influenced by the self-help sector, can impede authentic emotional reflection and exacerbate mental health issues such as anxiety and depression.

The self-help industry, in its pursuit of providing guidance, may inadvertently contribute to the decline of individual accountability.

By portraying success as a direct result of following specific strategies and failure as a consequence of not adhering to prescribed paths, individuals may externalize their control, attributing outcomes solely to external factors.

The dependence on extrinsic motivators, such as the prospect of achievement or the apprehension of defeat, can undermine intrinsic motivation—the inherent impetus that originates from personal gratification and a sense of meaning. The self-help industry's emphasis on external indicators of success may unintentionally diminish the profound influence of internal motivation on long-term personal growth.

Reports have emerged regarding exploitative practices in coaching and seminars within the self-help industry. People who are susceptible to the appeal of instant solutions may become trapped in costly programs that offer dramatic changes but provide little substance. Ethical concerns arise when the desire for profit takes precedence over the sincere intention to help individuals in their personal development process.

The widespread availability of self-help platforms, especially on the internet, exposes individuals to a plethora of advice, not all of which is well-founded or qualified. The spread of unverified or misleading information can present substantial dangers, potentially worsening current problems or guiding individuals towards unproductive courses of action.

A social media account suggests you have a voice that matters and 'staying in your lane' is a thing of the past.

Individuals who participate in the self-help industry are advised to approach its offerings with a critical mindset. Through careful analysis of the commitments made, comprehension of the constraints of universal solutions, and awareness of the business motives involved, individuals can make more knowledgeable choices regarding their personal growth goals.

Consumers, advocates, and industry professionals all share a collective responsibility to promote ethical practices in the self-help industry. This entails ensuring that practitioners are held responsible, advocating for openness, and cultivating a culture that places a higher value on the authentic welfare of individuals rather than profit-oriented incentives.

While receiving external guidance can be beneficial, it is crucial to complement it with internal introspection. It is important to acknowledge and appreciate the distinctiveness of each person's experiences, understand the intricacies of human psychology, and recognize the constraints of external interventions in order to promote a comprehensive approach to personal growth.

By addressing the unforeseen challenges of the self-help industry, people can foster a more sophisticated and genuine culture of personal development. This culture would value diversity, acknowledge the intricacies of the human journey, and prioritize the welfare of individuals over financial motives.

The self-help industry provides a wide range of resources for personal growth, but it also brings about various unintended issues that require thoughtful examination. The industry's impact extends beyond its intended purpose, encompassing the allure of expedient solutions, the erosion of personal accountability, and ethical considerations. To effectively navigate the overcrowded and shifting realm of self-help, one must possess a discerning mindset, critical thinking abilities, and an understanding of the potential drawbacks inherent in widely accepted stories of personal growth.

Chapter 4
Philosophy Isn't the Same as Self-Help

"The unexamined life is not worth living."
Socrates

Philosophy, originating from the Greek word "philosophia" which translates to "love of wisdom," is a methodical and analytical exploration of fundamental inquiries regarding reality, knowledge, values, reason, mind, and existence. Conversely, self-help generally pertains to a category of literature and methods focused on personal growth, providing advice on attaining particular objectives, surmounting obstacles, and improving overall welfare.

Ancient Greece serves as the origin of Western philosophy, where notable individuals such as Socrates, Plato, and Aristotle established the fundamental principles for organized investigation into the essence of existence, morality, and the human experience. Philosophical thought has progressed over time, encompassing different periods like the Renaissance, the Enlightenment, and existentialism, each adding to a diverse range of ideas and perspectives.

Philosophy has thrived in various cultural contexts outside of the Western tradition, encompassing Confucianism and Daoism in China, as well as Vedanta and Nyaya in India. Every tradition offers distinct perspectives on matters of existence, morality, and the essence of reality, thereby enriching the worldwide conversation on the human condition.

Metaphysics is a fundamental field of philosophy that explores inquiries regarding the essence of reality, existence, and the interconnection between consciousness and physical substance. Philosophers delve into profound investigations concerning subjects such as the essence of existence, causality, and the fundamental organization of the cosmos.

Epistemology is the field of study that examines knowledge and delves into inquiries regarding belief, justification, and the essence of truth. The philosophers in this discipline aim to comprehend the process by which we acquire knowledge, scrutinizing the fundamental principles of knowledge and the boundaries of human comprehension.

Ethics is a fundamental discipline within philosophy that deals with moral inquiries, exploring notions such as righteousness and wickedness, excellence and depravity, and the principles that govern ethical choices. Philosophers explore the fundamental principles of ethical frameworks and the essence of moral accountability.

Logic, an essential discipline within philosophy, centers on the fundamental principles of sound reasoning and argumentation. Philosophers in this discipline scrutinize the framework of arguments, explore logical errors, and contribute to the advancement of rational techniques for assessing assertions and statements.

Philosophy books targeted at the general public have experienced a significant increase in popularity in recent years. Although the increased accessibility of philosophical ideas has allowed them to reach a wider audience, it has also led to a misconception: the belief that philosophy is a type of self-improvement. The titles "The Art of Happiness" and "The Philosophy of Well-Being" imply a merging of philosophical exploration with practical guidance for individual growth.

Amidst an age marked by an excessive amount of information and the dominance of concise statements, intricate philosophical concepts are frequently condensed into simplified, easily digestible fragments to cater to a wide audience. Although the ease of access to philosophical concepts can be advantageous, it can also lead to the misconception that philosophy is mainly focused on providing immediate resolutions to the difficulties of life.

Self-help literature commonly focuses on providing practical advice and concrete strategies to attain specific goals. Self-help books frequently offer a clear plan for individuals who desire concrete enhancements in various aspects of their lives, such as relationships, career achievements, or mental well-being.

The core of self-help literature revolves around an approach that focuses on the individual, emphasizing personal empowerment, self-exploration, and the achievement of personal objectives. The genre frequently motivates readers to assume control over their lives and implement constructive modifications through distinct strategies and practices.

Several self-help books incorporate accounts of personal metamorphosis and triumph, frequently utilizing the experiences of individuals who have surmounted hardship or accomplished noteworthy objectives (think "Can't Hurt Me" by David Goggins). These narratives function as inspirational anecdotes designed to inspire readers to replicate comparable routes to achievement.

Contrary to the simplistic view of philosophy as a tool for personal improvement, authentic philosophical investigation functions as a means of introspection rather than offering specific guidance. Philosophical texts prompt readers to confront difficult concepts, urging them to scrutinize presuppositions, evaluate reasoning, and participate in profound reflection.

Engaging in the study of philosophy fosters the development of critical thinking and analytical abilities. Philosophers undergo training to assess arguments, detect logical fallacies, and participate in rigorous discussions. These skills enhance one's intellectual repertoire, but they diverge from the pragmatic, objective-driven emphasis commonly found in self-help literature.

Philosophical exploration of ethics offers a structured approach to tackling important moral dilemmas and scrutinizing the principles that govern ethical choices. Philosophy promotes the examination of the moral aspects of one's decisions and behaviors, rather than providing direct solutions.

Philosophical concepts possess an inherent resistance to being overly simplified. Efforts to simplify incredibly complex philosophical ideas into clear-cut principles may lead to a reduction in subtlety and profundity. Philosophical inquiry flourishes through the examination of ambiguity, paradox, and the indefinite nature of fundamental questions.

Contrary to self-help literature, which frequently offers straightforward answers, philosophy recognizes the intricate nature of human experience. Philosophers acknowledge that inquiries regarding existence, morality, and knowledge lack universally applicable solutions. The process of philosophical inquiry entails embracing ambiguity and actively engaging with the complexities of various viewpoints.

A fundamental difference between philosophy and self-help lies in the inherent significance of philosophical investigation. Philosophers engage in the pursuit of wisdom not only for practical benefits but also as a goal in its own right. The inherent worth resides in the act of interrogating, investigating, and actively participating in the profound enigmas of existence.

Philosophy provides the pleasure of engaging in intellectual investigation, delving into the extensive realm of concepts that have influenced societies over time. Self-help literature offers practical techniques for immediate use, whereas philosophy invites individuals to embark on a lifelong quest for intellectual exploration, fostering a profound comprehension of the intricacies of human existence.

Philosophy is an essential component of a comprehensive education. It fosters the growth of individuals' comprehensive outlook, refining their capacity to think critically, evaluate arguments, and interact with various philosophical lineages. A philosophical education enhances the development of knowledgeable, introspective individuals who are adept at navigating the intricacies of a globalized society.

Although philosophy is not a type of self-help, it remains pertinent to daily existence. Philosophical concepts can enhance the process of making ethical decisions, cultivate analytical thinking in resolving problems, and contribute to a more profound comprehension of the human condition. Nevertheless, this significance is based on the development of sagacity rather than the quest for immediate pragmatic resolutions.

Philosophy functions as a tool for introspection, stimulating individuals to interrogate presuppositions, confront prejudices, and contemplate alternative viewpoints. Interacting with philosophical texts can result in an increased consciousness of one's convictions and principles, promoting intellectual modesty and a readiness to confront the intricacies of existence.

Self-help literature may offer prescriptive guidance, but philosophy provides practical wisdom by offering a nuanced comprehension of life's intricacies. Practical wisdom encompasses the capacity to effectively handle moral predicaments, form rational decisions, and acknowledge the inherent uncertainties of human existence. Epistemic understanding arises from deliberate contemplation rather than adherence to a predetermined sequence of actions.

There is a need for society to have a greater understanding of philosophy in order to distinguish it from self-help. A society that has a deep understanding of philosophical investigation is more capable of dealing with ethical dilemmas, participating in well-informed public discussions, and valuing the various viewpoints that enrich the intellectual and cultural environment.

Philosophical education is crucial for developing and nurturing critical thinking abilities. Education in philosophy cultivates intellectual resilience and a willingness to consider diverse perspectives by instructing individuals in the skills of argument analysis, distinguishing between valid and fallacious reasoning, and understanding the intricacies of philosophical texts.

To have an informed citizenry, people need to comprehend fundamental philosophical concepts. Philosophy provides individuals with the necessary skills to analyze societal norms, challenge authority, and actively participate in well-informed civic discussions. Amidst the various ethical and existential dilemmas that our world faces, possessing philosophical literacy becomes a valuable tool for cultivating conscientious citizenship.

To summarize, regarding philosophy as a means of personal improvement oversimplifies the profound profundity and intricacy inherent in philosophical investigation. Although philosophy and self-help both aim to facilitate personal growth, they differ in their methodologies, objectives, and the type of knowledge they provide. Philosophy, originating from a deep appreciation for wisdom, beckons individuals to embark on a voyage of intellectual investigation and contemplation—a voyage that goes beyond the immediate quest for practical resolutions.

The enduring significance of philosophy lies in its ability to enhance lives by fostering wisdom, analytical reasoning, and a more profound comprehension of the human condition. When individuals delve into philosophy, they set out on a journey to intellectually explore, question assumptions, and embrace the inherent intricacies of existence.

Developing a sophisticated comprehension of philosophy entails acknowledging its differentiation from self-help while recognizing its significance in a comprehensive education and a thriving society. By promoting an ongoing discussion on philosophical investigation, society can surpass misunderstandings and embrace the intrinsic worth of philosophy as a field that goes beyond seeking immediate practical resolutions.

Chapter 5
Absurdism

"The realization that life is absurd cannot be an end, but only a beginning. This is a truth nearly all great minds have taken as their starting
point."
Albert Camus

I n the 20th century, there was a significant change in philosophical
thinking with the emergence of absurdism. This philosophical
movement focused on the fundamental lack of meaning and purpose
that used to be regarded as inherent in the human experience. Albert
Camus, a prominent figure in the field of absurdism, played a leading
role in this existential investigation and significantly influenced the
intellectual sphere. This chapter seeks to explore the origins of Absurdism, examining its foundations and highlighting the significant
impact of Albert Camus on this philosophical movement.

Prior to discussing absurdism, it is essential to situate its origin
within the wider framework of existential philosophy. The absurdist
movement was built upon the foundation of existentialism, which, as
I previously mentioned, prioritizes individual freedom and responsibility. Visionaries such as Jean-Paul Sartre and Søren Kierkegaard
challenged conventional ideas about the meaning and purpose of life
in a world that appeared to lack concrete answers for either.

The examination of the human condition by existentialists provided a conducive environment for the development of absurdism. The absurdist movement represents a logical advancement, challenging the limits of existential philosophy to address the inherent paradoxes of human existence.

The formalization of absurdism as a distinct philosophical stance can be attributed to the works of Albert Camus. The term "absurd" succinctly captures the inherent contradiction between humanity's inherent pursuit of significance and the apparent lack of meaning in the universe. In his influential essay "The Myth of Sisyphus," Camus elaborates on the inherent absurdity of the human condition, positioning it as a fundamental principle within his philosophical framework.

"The Myth of Sisyphus" by Camus introduces the mythological character Sisyphus, who is condemned to perpetually push a large rock up a hill, only for it to repeatedly roll back down. Camus argues that the sense of meaninglessness in existence serves as a metaphor for the human quest for purpose in a universe that, in his view, shows no concern for our desires, wishes, attention, etc.

Camus argues that recognizing the inherent meaninglessness of existence does not advocate for nihilism, but rather encourages individuals to wholeheartedly embrace and engage with life. The central theme in most of Camus's works is the act of defying the absurd by choosing to live authentically, even though life lacks inherent meaning.

In "The Rebel," Camus expands upon his absurdist philosophy by examining rebellion as a reaction to the absurd. When confronted with an apparently indifferent and cold universe, rebellion serves as a means of asserting one's personal autonomy and honor.

Camus's concept of rebellion is not a thoughtless resistance to authority, but rather a sophisticated and principled act of challenging unjust systems and the inherent irrationality of the human condition. The ethical position of absurdism sets it apart from mere existential distress.

Although absurdism shares thematic elements with nihilism and existentialism, Camus differentiates his philosophy from these counterparts. Camus criticizes nihilism for its passive resignation due to its complete rejection of meaning. Existentialism, however, is criticized for its inclination to fabricate artificial significance in a seemingly apathetic cosmos.

Camus's philosophy promotes an assertive engagement with the absurd, rejecting both the passive nihilistic resignation and the artificial constructs of existential significance. The proposal suggests a genuine involvement with the inherent contradictions of life and a defiance against the irrationality of existence.

Camus delves into the concept of absurdism not only in his philosophical essays but also in his literary works, particularly "The Stranger" and "The Plague." He effectively depicts the irrationality of human existence and the ethical quandaries that emerge when confronted with the irrational, using his characters' experiences.

"The Stranger" ("L'Étranger" in French) by Albert Camus is a philosophical novel that explores the mysterious existence of its main character, Meursault. The novel, published in 1942, is a fundamental work of absurdist literature, which arose during the post-war era and aimed to challenge the significance and objective of life in a seemingly apathetic universe.

It is a stark depiction of the life of Meursault, an Algerian clerk residing in French Algiers, who is characterized by his emotional detachment and apathy. The story commences with the announcement of his mother's demise, and right from the outset, his absence of emotional reaction becomes evident. The novel subsequently traces his impassive odyssey through existence, exploring the themes of existentialism, the absurd, and the repercussions of detached existence.

As I mentioned above, Meursault's character is characterized by his emotional aloofness and apathy. He maintains a detached role as an observer in his own life, consistently refusing to adhere to societal norms regarding sorrow, affection, or ethical principles. He exhibits a nearly detached and objective demeanor when reacting to various events in his life, such as the aforementioned passing of his mother and his participation in a homicide.

The concept of the absurd lies at the very essence of Meursault's existence. Absurdism asserts that life is inherently devoid of meaning, and the pursuit of rationality or purpose is ultimately pointless, but we shouldn't just merely give up or give in to passive nihilism. Meursault personifies the concept of the absurd by maneuvering through a society that requires emotional involvement and moral assessments, despite his indifference towards these societal expectations, but he stumbles when it comes to the possibility of living for something, anything.

The novel is set in the intense heat of the Algerian summer, which serves as an unyielding and apathetic natural setting that reflects the absurdity of Meursault's life. The relentless and unyielding nature of the absurd is emphasized by the unforgiving sun, which serves as a metaphor for the harsh and indifferent universe in which Meursault lives.

The trial of Meursault exemplifies the absurdity inherent in the judicial system (something Kafka did as well in a different absurdist novel). The attention transitions from the concrete criminal act to Meursault's perceived ethical deficiencies, including his absence of sorrow during his mother's funeral, his emotional detachment, and his defiance of societal conventions. The trial underscores the capricious and illogical essence of the justice system, adding to the overarching theme of absurdity.

The relationship between Meursault and Marie serves as a symbol of the irrationality of love. Their relationship is superficial, primarily based on physical attraction rather than emotional intimacy. Meursault's apathy towards the possibility of marriage and his nonchalant attitude towards relationships bolster the notion that in an irrational world, conventional concepts of love and dedication carry minimal importance.

Meursault's association with Raymond, a morally dubious individual, demonstrates a deeper sense of the irrationality of traditional moral standards. Meursault's impartial embrace of Raymond's conduct, encompassing domestic violence, defies societal norms, thereby exemplifying the novel's central motif of the capriciousness of moral evaluations.

The climax of Meursault's journey is characterized by the apparently irrational homicide of an Arab individual on a shoreline. The action itself lacks any motive or rationality, highlighting the irrationality of violence in a world that lacks inherent significance. The novel's examination of the irrationality of human behavior is further underscored by Meursault's emotional detachment both during and after the act.

The ultimate clash between Meursault and the prison chaplain provides a poignant examination of the absurdity within the realm of religion. Meursault, an atheist, refuses the chaplain's endeavors to offer him spiritual comfort and purpose in his existence. The scene highlights the inherent conflict between religious narratives and the absurdist worldview, which emphasizes the need to construct meaning rather than passively accepting it.

Meursault's expedition, characterized by emotional disengagement and a rejection of societal norms, epitomizes the senselessness of navigating a world lacking inherent significance. The novel prompts readers to confront the existential emptiness and wrestle with the consequences of a universe that is indifferent to human matters, an idea that is oddly unpopular in the 21st century due to gurus and movements that suggest you can merely manifest anything you want because the universe cares that much about you.

"The Plague" another absurdist novel by Albert Camus, known as "La Peste" in French, is a profound examination of the human condition when confronted with an unexplainable and devastating epidemic. The novel, published in 1947, explores the town of Oran, Algeria, as it confronts an abrupt outbreak of a plague that disrupts the normal patterns of daily existence. Camus employs this narrative to elucidate the inherent irrationality of human existence, the inescapability of anguish, and the pursuit of significance in a seemingly apathetic cosmos.

"The Plague" commences in the Algerian town of Oran with the enigmatic manifestation of deceased rodents. Shortly after, the town is hit by an epidemic, and Dr. Bernard Rieux becomes the narrator and a key figure. The story progresses through his written accounts, documenting the town's collective reaction to the plague, the challenges faced by individuals, and the underlying philosophical concepts that form the basis of the narrative.

Dr. Rieux, serving as both a central character and narrator, personifies the absurdist viewpoint. His commitment to providing medical care to the ill and fighting against the spread of the plague is characterized by a resilient acknowledgment of the senselessness of human affliction. Rieux faces the plague not by searching for significance, but by dedicating himself to relieving the immediate anguish of those impacted.

Te abrupt and unmanageable epidemic of the plague in Oran functions as an absurdist analogy for the capricious and irrational essence of human affliction. The epidemic disrupts the regularity of daily life, revealing the vulnerability of human existence when confronted with incomprehensible forces.

The novel's beginning, characterized by the unexplainable demise of rodents, prefigures the imminent outbreak of a deadly epidemic. Rats, as vectors of disease, symbolize the irrational and uncontrollable facets of existence. The recurrent pattern of the plague, with its unpredictable occurrence and withdrawal, highlights the inherent irrationality of human efforts to combat inexplicable forces.

The town of Oran, initially exhibiting denial towards the gravity of the plague, exemplifies the innate human inclination to resist acknowledging the irrationality of suffering. The town's leaders endeavor to justify the unexplainable, reflecting society's inclination to seek significance even when confronted with irrational occurrences.

Rambert, a journalist who is estranged from his wife due to the quarantine, personifies the innate human inclination to defy the senselessness of anguish. The individual's unwavering determination to find a way out symbolizes the fruitless search for purpose and normality in a world that has been disrupted by the irrationality of the plague.

Cottard, a dubious individual who flourishes in the midst of the plague, adjusts to the irrationality by wholeheartedly accepting the disorder. His adeptness in maneuvering through irrational situations and capitalizing on the misfortune of others exemplifies an alternative approach to the absurd, characterized by opportunism and a disregard for moral boundaries.

Dr. Rieux's dedication to fighting the plague exemplifies the principles of absurdist philosophy. He does not act with a desire to find meaning or a belief in a higher purpose. Instead, he recognizes the inherent irrationality of the situation and responds by dedicating himself pragmatically to reducing suffering.

Rieux's portrayal as a "absurd hero" corresponds with Camus's examination of heroism in the presence of the absurd. Rieux's heroism is characterized by a steadfast dedication to directly and tangibly relieving human suffering, rather than through extravagant actions or a search for abstract significance.

Father Paneloux, the Jesuit priest of the town, initially perceives the plague as a divine retribution. The sermons he delivers promote a religious approach, presenting the suffering as a trial of one's faith. Nevertheless, as the plague progresses, Paneloux's conviction falters, and he grapples with the constraints of religious justifications when confronted with incomprehensible affliction.

Camus, a critic of religious transcendence, examines the irrationality of divine silence in the face of human suffering. The plague poses a challenge to conventional religious narratives that aim to offer significance and direction in the midst of hardship. The lack of divine intervention serves as evidence for the absurdist viewpoint.

Ultimately, "The Plague" functions as a profound examination of the inherent irrationality present in the human experience. Albert Camus, in his exploration of the plague, constructs a story that questions traditional ideas about significance, ethics, and the quest for transcendence. The characters in the novel struggle with the illogical and random essence of pain, mirroring Camus's wider philosophical investigations into the absurd.

Camus's literary works not only serve as artistic representations of absurdism but also effectively communicate important philosophical concepts to a wider range of readers. Camus employs literature as a means to prompt readers to directly confront the irrationality and meaninglessness of life in a deeply felt and emotional manner.

Albert Camus's philosophical legacy endures as a cornerstone of absurdism, continuing to influence existential thought and literary discourse. His deep understanding of the human condition, combined with his exceptional writing skills, establish him as a significant figure in the development and expression of absurdism.

Following Camus's contributions, absurdism continues to be a vibrant and developing philosophical school of thought, encouraging ongoing investigation and reinterpretation. The impact of Albert Camus extends beyond academic spheres and permeates the wider cultural awareness, serving as a reminder for humanity to bravely confront the inherent meaninglessness of life, rebel against it, and steadfastly pursue a genuine and true way of living.

Chapter 6
Embrace the Irrational

"The greatest obstacle to living is expectancy, which hangs upon to-morrow and loses today. The whole future lies in uncertainty: live immediately."

Seneca

Within the complex fabric of human life, one aspect that is frequently disregarded is the embracing of the absurd, or the *irrationality of life* if we don't want to use a philosophical label even though the two are somewhat interchangeable. This chapter undertakes a deep exploration into the profound notion that embracing life's inherent irrationality and acknowledging the impossibility of rationalizing everything can lead to a more meaningful and fulfilling existence. By utilizing philosophical analysis and psychological viewpoints, I aim to reveal how accepting the irrational can lead to resilience, creativity, and a deep sense of satisfaction.

The human condition is a fusion of various encounters, sentiments, and connections, frequently surpassing clear classification and logical elucidation. The non-rational aspects of our existence, such as the unexplainable aesthetic appeal of art or the profound intensity of certain emotions, defy the limitations of logical explanation. Acknowledging the existence of irrationality in our lives is the initial stage in embracing the abundance that arises from recognizing the intricacy that lies beyond the limits of pure rationality.

The irrational, rather than being a disruptive force, can be perceived as a constructive one. It prompts us to question our existing beliefs and encourages us to investigate unfamiliar territory, cultivating a feeling of awe and inquisitiveness. This acknowledgement establishes the foundation for a comprehensive comprehension of human nature and a profound bond with the capricious forces of existence.

Although rational thinking is crucial for navigating the world, it does have inherent limitations. The inclination to enforce rationality in all aspects of existence can result in frustration and a feeling of existential dissatisfaction. The complex and diverse nature of life is difficult to categorize accurately, and trying to fit it into a rigid rational framework can lead to a simplified and limited understanding.

Recognizing the boundaries of rationality does not imply embracing irrationality as disorder, but rather extends an invitation to value the complex subtleties that lie outside the realm of reason. This statement recognizes that certain aspects of existence elude simple explanations and that the human journey is inherently complicated and diverse.

The nature of life is inherently unpredictable, and striving to eliminate all unpredictability through inflexible rational systems is an impossible and futile endeavor. By accepting the irrationality and unpredictability of life, individuals can more effectively navigate through periods of uncertainty. This acceptance cultivates resilience, empowering individuals to adjust to unexpected circumstances and discover significance even in the presence of uncertainty.

Embracing uncertainty allows individuals to utilize resilience and adaptability to shape the course of their lives. Instead of being afraid of what is not known, individuals who accept the illogical elements of uncertainty discover the liberty to investigate, acquire knowledge, and develop amidst life's unpredictability.

Significant advancements in human history have often emerged from the domain of the irrational. Creativity frequently arises when individuals liberate their minds to venture beyond the limitations of rigid rationality. Embracing irrationality allows for the exploration of new possibilities, original concepts, and unconventional approaches to pressing issues.

The annals of human accomplishment abound with examples where individuals boldly challenged the prevailing rational conventions of their era. The embrace of the irrational has played a crucial role in driving progress, from artistic revolutions that questioned traditional viewpoints to scientific breakthroughs that challenged established paradigms.

An important component of accepting the irrational entails acknowledging and comprehending emotions that defy logical justification. Emotions, frequently characterized by irrationality, have a vital impact on the human experience. Enhancing emotional intelligence, which involves understanding and managing one's own emotions as well as perceiving and comprehending the emotions of others, enhances the quality and depth of interpersonal relationships. The spirit of the age we're currently living in suggests that emotions should be drivers instead of navigators. This, of course, is causing more harm than good.

Emotional intelligence, based on recognizing the illogical nature of emotions, enables individuals to navigate the ever-changing landscape of human relationships with empathy and comprehension. It cultivates a more profound bond with others and improves the overall standard of living by surpassing the constraints of rigid rationality.

Life is abundant with paradoxes that defy simple rationalization. Recognizing and inviting paradoxes provides individuals with a deeper comprehension of the complexities of human existence. Embracing paradoxical elements can result in a more sophisticated perspective, enabling the integration of conflicting concepts and promoting cognitive and spiritual development.

Paradoxes, when accepted and understood for what they are, serve as portals to profound understanding and sagacity. They encourage individuals to surpass dualistic thinking and recognize the intricacy inherent in the human experience (not everything is black or white even though we're told it is). Embracing paradoxes fosters a mindset that is receptive and adaptable when dealing with the intricacies of existence.

Mindfulness, which involves recognizing the current moment without making judgments, closely corresponds to accepting irrationality. Mindfulness promotes the act of observing thoughts and emotions without the intention of rationalizing or exerting control over them (*I'm thinking this way for a reason. What is that reason?*). This impartial consciousness fosters a feeling of tranquility and satisfaction, surpassing the perpetual requirement for logical justification.

Practicing mindfulness entails fostering a close connection with the current moment, recognizing and accepting both the logical and illogical elements of one's own experience. This practice enables individuals to disengage from the constant and repetitive thoughts of the logical mind and establish a profound and instinctive comprehension of life.

Various philosophical traditions, including existentialism and Eastern philosophies, have extensively dealt with the intricacies of human existence, recognizing the constraints of rationality. Existentialist philosophers, such as the ones I've already discussed, highlighted the irrationality of specific elements of human existence and advocated for personal autonomy in response to the inherent uncertainties of life.

The vast array of philosophical ideas offers individuals various viewpoints on accepting the irrational. Philosophy provides numerous avenues for individuals to delve into the correlation between reason and the irrational, ranging from the existentialist plea for authenticity in the face of life's absurdity to the Eastern focus on equilibrium and harmony.

Psychologically, accepting the irrational is consistent with the principles of cognitive-behavioral therapy and positive psychology. Acceptance and Commitment Therapy (ACT), for instance, promotes the acceptance of one's thoughts and feelings without evaluation, thereby cultivating psychological adaptability and resilience.

An individual's psychological well-being is closely connected to their capacity to navigate the irrational aspects of their experience. Approaches such as cognitive-behavioral therapy acknowledge the inherent irrationality of specific thoughts and emotions. They provide individuals with practical techniques to effectively handle and embrace these aspects without being overwhelmed by discomfort.

Ultimately, embracing the irrational becomes a fundamental principle for leading a fulfilling life. Through acknowledging the boundaries of rationality, embracing uncertainty, and recognizing the influence of emotions, individuals can develop resilience, creativity, and emotional intelligence. Engaging with contradictions and nurturing awareness additionally enhances a deeper and more significant existence.

Embracing the irrational perspective can transform the pursuit of a fulfilling life into a voyage of self-exploration and individual development. The recognition that not all things can be easily rationalized or controlled (a stoic idea we'll cover later) encourages individuals to undertake a journey towards self-awareness, comprehension, and acceptance.

Embracing the irrational aspects of one's life allows for the exploration of self-discovery, an ongoing journey towards comprehending one's values, beliefs, and aspirations. This process of self-discovery is characterized by a readiness to confront the intricacies within oneself, recognizing both the logical and illogical elements that influence personal identity.

Self-discovery is a crucial aspect of personal development, as individuals explore the complex landscape of their emotions, desires, and motivations. By accepting and embracing the irrational, individuals can gain a more profound comprehension of their own strengths and vulnerabilities, which in turn cultivates resilience when confronted with the difficulties of life.

The path of life is filled with obstacles, uncertainties, and unforeseen twists. Embracing irrationality provides individuals with the necessary resilience to navigate these situations. Being able to embrace and adjust to unexpected situations, instead of being immobilized by the requirement for logical justifications, becomes a reservoir of resilience.

Resilience, developed by embracing the irrational, enables individuals to recover from setbacks, gain knowledge from experiences, and embrace the transformative aspect of challenges. It is an inherent characteristic that enables personal development even when confronted with challenges.

Human relationships possess an inherent complexity that frequently eludes rational analysis. By accepting the illogical elements of interpersonal dynamics, individuals can effectively navigate relationships with empathy and compassion. Recognizing that emotions, whether logical or illogical, have a significant impact on relationships, promotes the development of more profound and more significant connections.

Within the domain of personal relationships, embracing irrationality has the potential to bring about profound change. It promotes individuals to address conflicts with empathy, recognize the distinctiveness of others, and establish connections that surpass the boundaries of mere logical compatibility.

The societal expectation to adhere to rational standards of success, beauty, and accomplishment frequently results in an ongoing quest for flawlessness. By embracing irrationality, individuals free themselves from the limitations imposed by unrealistic standards, enabling them to live a more genuine and satisfying life.

The recognition that flaws and uncertainties are inherent facets of the human condition redirects attention from an unachievable standard to a more practical and comprehensive one. This transition fosters self-acknowledgement and an authentic admiration for the varied mosaic of human experiences.

Well-being encompasses a comprehensive approach to physical, mental, and emotional health, going beyond the mere absence of illness. Embracing irrationality enhances one's holistic comprehension of well-being, highlighting the significance of equilibrium, self-preservation, and adaptability.

Adopting a comprehensive approach to well-being entails fostering the mental, physical, and spiritual aspects, acknowledging that each component contributes to the overall standard of life. Embracing the irrational is an essential element in this comprehensive framework, enabling individuals to fully embrace the entire range of human experiences.

Embracing the irrational aspects of life transforms the journey into a search for significance rather than an unyielding pursuit of solutions. The focus transitions from a mindset centered on reaching a specific destination to an acknowledgment of the abundance discovered within the journey itself.

Discovering significance in the journey entails relishing the current moment, fostering appreciation for the varied encounters experienced, and embracing the uncertainties that inherently give depth to life. The invitation of the irrational into your life serves as a guiding tenet, reminding individuals that significance is frequently unearthed amidst life's uncertainties.

To summarize, embracing irrationality becomes a catalyst for personal growth and fulfillment. By engaging in self-exploration, demonstrating resilience, fostering meaningful relationships, letting go of the pursuit of perfection, adopting a comprehensive approach to well-being, and seeking purpose in life's experiences, individuals can gracefully and genuinely navigate the intricacies of human existence.

Leading a fulfilling existence surpasses the inflexible boundaries of strict rationality, encouraging individuals to embrace the inherent intricacies and uncertainties. The embrace of irrationality serves as a guiding principle, leading individuals to a deeper comprehension of their own selves, their connections with others, and the complex fabric of existence. As we embrace irrationality, we realize that its unpredictability holds the potential for a meaningful, connected, and truly fulfilling life.

Chapter 7
Discovering Purpose in the Pointless

"A man can't live without some reason for living. It's intolerable to be told there's no reason for existing."
Albert Camus

Within the vast scope of human existence, individuals frequently encounter situations where the search for significance appears to be a difficult illusion, and purpose seems to fade away into a seemingly meaningless void. This chapter delves into a detailed examination of finding purpose in the midst of apparent meaninglessness. We explore existential philosophy, psychology, and narratives of resilience to understand how individuals can navigate prolonged periods of existential ambiguity and, despite challenges, develop a deep sense of purpose.

The existentialist philosophy, eloquently expounded by renowned figures like Albert Camus and Jean-Paul Sartre, confronts the deep sense of absurdity that is inherent in human existence. The absurd arises when individuals, driven by an inherent longing for logical significance, confront a universe that, occasionally, appears apathetic or even antagonistic towards such endeavors. The acknowledgment of life's absurdity transforms from a mere philosophical perspective into a fundamental assumption for understanding the complex difficulties of discovering meaning in seemingly purposeless situations.

Existential ambiguity serves as a platform for evaluating the human spirit, compelling individuals to confront the boundaries of conventional frameworks that typically provide guidance in their quest for meaning. Recognizing the inherent senselessness of life, instead of causing a sense of hopelessness, prompts a desire for profound introspection and the establishment of individual significance.

Existential ambiguity is a complex condition in which individuals struggle with the lack of distinct meaning or purpose. During these instances, traditional systems that usually offer direction fail, leaving individuals stranded in a state of ambiguity. Existential thinkers contend that facing this inherent uncertainty is not a futile endeavor, but rather a priceless chance for deep introspection and the development of individual significance in the presence of seeming purposelessness.

As people navigate through this complex and uncertain situation, they are encouraged to contemplate their own existence, the principles they cherish, and the growing network of relationships that shape their lives. The investigation of existential ambiguity becomes a profound voyage that surpasses the mere pursuit of external significance, prompting individuals to utilize internal capabilities and generate purpose from within.

Resilience, which refers to the ability to recover from difficulties, is crucial in finding meaning in situations that may appear meaningless. Individuals who demonstrate resilience in the face of existential challenges possess an exceptional capacity to adjust, acquire knowledge, and derive profound significance from their encounters. The development of psychological resilience through such experiences becomes a crucial characteristic, allowing individuals to navigate the inherent uncertainties in the pursuit of meaning.

To embark on the path of purposefulness, one must possess a strong ability to persevere through obstacles, gain knowledge from mistakes, and stay resolute when confronted with uncertainty about the meaning of life. Resilience is a dynamic attribute that enables personal development even in extremely challenging circumstances. It serves as the basis for individuals to create a purposeful story from the seemingly disordered and purposeless aspects of their existence.

Examining personal narratives is a crucial method for comprehending how individuals have discovered meaning in the midst of existential difficulties. Case studies and autobiographical accounts provide a diverse range of experiences, offering valuable insights into how individuals can find deep significance in seemingly meaningless situations.

These narratives act as guiding lights, leading others through the intricacies of their own existential quests. Through analyzing the narratives of individuals who have navigated through the realm of futility and emerged with a clear sense of direction, people can acquire motivation, tactics, and a guide for their own pursuits of significance. Personal narratives serve as more than just anecdotal evidence; they act as a repository of collective wisdom, demonstrating that purpose can indeed be found in situations that may initially appear devoid of meaning.

Psychological studies on the quest for happiness and well-being highlight the significance of intrinsic meaning, which refers to a sense of purpose that comes from within oneself rather than being imposed by external factors. Uncovering inherent significance entails a deep synchronization of individual principles, interests, and abilities with one's behaviors and decisions in life. Engaging in introspection serves as a reliable tool for finding direction in a world lacking purpose, providing individuals with a trustworthy guide amidst the chaotic uncertainty of existence.

Discovering inherent significance necessitates a purposeful and self-reflective analysis of one's convictions, longings, and ambitions. It involves developing self-awareness, which allows individuals to identify the aspects that align with their true selves. The inherent significance of something serves as a stabilizing influence, providing individuals with a sense of purpose that goes beyond the temporary and external changes in life.

The creative process serves as a potent catalyst for uncovering purpose in the midst of apparent meaninglessness. Participating in creative endeavors, be it in the realms of art, science, or business, enables individuals to surpass the constraints of traditional thought. The act of creation not only provides inherent meaning but also serves as a means to find purpose when predetermined significance is lacking.

Creativity cultivates a broad and flexible mindset, enabling individuals to perceive their existence with a perspective of potential rather than limitation. The inherent ability to innovate in creative pursuits serves as a guiding light for discovering purpose, providing new opportunities to create meaning in the face of existential difficulties. Creativity, whether expressed through art, science, or entrepreneurship, becomes a powerful force in the pursuit of purpose.

Existential courage, as promoted by existentialist philosophers, entails accepting the duty to generate significance in the presence of life's intrinsic lack of meaning. Living authentically, marked by introspection and a dedication to one's principles, becomes a fundamental aspect in finding meaning amidst the seemingly purposeless. This existential bravery compels individuals to directly face the emptiness and actively mold their futures.

True authenticity necessitates a profound self-honesty, surpassing societal norms and external influences. It requires the bravery to challenge, to select, and to create significance in accordance with one's principles and convictions. Existential courage emerges as the primary motivator for purposeful living amidst the uncertainty of existence, compelling individuals to transcend the ordinary and actively confront the profound inquiries of being.

The involvement and relationships within a community are crucial in the process of finding one's purpose. Participating in significant interpersonal connections and making valuable contributions to a broader social framework establishes a structure for living with intention and purpose. The communal aspect of purpose discovery underscores the interdependent nature of human existence, surpassing individual pursuits for significance.

Amidst a network of human relationships, we find chances for mutual understanding and cooperative objectives. The interaction between our individual pursuits for meaning and the collective environment becomes a dynamic and influential power, enhancing the overall tapestry of life. The communal nature of purpose discovery serves as a reminder that meaning, even in the presence of futility, is frequently found and cultivated within the framework of collective human encounters.

Existential despair, characterized by a deep feeling of hopelessness resulting from the belief that life lacks meaning, necessitates the use of adaptive coping mechanisms. Engaging in therapeutic methods, such as existential psychotherapy, mindfulness, and acceptance, equips individuals with strategies to manage the emotional difficulties that arise when seeking meaning in seemingly futile situations.

Strategies for dealing with existential despair encompass a comprehensive approach that tackles the emotional, cognitive, and behavioral aspects of the human experience. Existential psychotherapy, which is based on philosophical investigation, provides individuals with an opportunity to examine their existential worries and create a unique storyline that infuses life with significance. Mindfulness practices, which focus on being fully aware of the present moment, can be a valuable tool for coping with the intense emotional distress that comes with existential despair. Acceptance, as a mechanism for dealing with difficult situations, entails recognizing the inherent unpredictability of life and adopting a mindset that embraces these uncertainties without giving in to feelings of hopelessness.

Existential psychotherapy, based on the principles of existential philosophers, serves as a guiding principle for individuals navigating the complex depths of existential despair. Through engaging in reflective discourse and self-examination, individuals have the ability to confront their most profound fears and concerns, thereby gradually converting existential hopelessness into a chance for self-realization and personal development.

Mindfulness practices, such as meditation and mindful breathing, equip individuals with practical techniques to navigate the emotional turbulence linked to existential despair. Through the practice of maintaining a state of open-mindedness and acceptance towards their thoughts and emotions, individuals can enhance their ability to remain calm and composed when confronted with the unpredictable aspects of life. Mindfulness serves as a sanctuary, enabling individuals to ground themselves in the current moment and discover comfort amidst the existential turmoil.

Acceptance, as a method of dealing with difficulties, entails a deep recognition of the fundamental uncertainties that exist in life. Instead of opposing or negating the apparent futility that may be prevalent, individuals have the option to accept the ambiguity and discover significance in the process of maneuvering through it. Acceptance is a powerful position that enables individuals to rise above existential despair and actively engage in shaping their own sense of purpose.

In conclusion, the process of uncovering meaning in seemingly meaningless situations is a complex endeavor that encompasses the fields of philosophy, psychology, creativity, resilience, and community. The concepts of existence, ambiguity in the nature of existence, personal stories, inherent significance, creativity, bravery in the face of existential challenges, social bonds, and methods for dealing with feelings of existential hopelessness together create a complex pattern that helps us navigate through the maze of meaninglessness.

As we navigate the complicated realm of existential uncertainty, we are encouraged to contemplate the deep lessons of existential philosophy, finding inspiration from those who have discovered meaning in the midst of apparent insignificance. Resilience is a powerful force that allows us to recover from difficult situations and find significance, even in the face of adversity. Personal narratives shed light on the various methods through which individuals can uncover their purpose, providing a plethora of valuable perspectives for those of us embarking on our own journeys to find meaning.

The quest for inherent significance serves as a guide, leading us to synchronize our values with their actions and embark on a voyage of self-exploration. Creativity serves as a catalyst for discovering one's purpose and allows for the creation of new ways to find meaning when faced with existential difficulties. Existential courage serves as the motivating factor, enabling us to confront the emptiness and actively determine our futures.

The significance of communal meaning-making highlights the crucial role of collective human experiences in the pursuit of purpose. Participating in significant relationships and making contributions to a broader societal context offer individuals a structure for purposeful existence that goes beyond personal endeavors. Strategies for dealing with existential despair provide practical methods for handling the emotional intricacies linked to the perceived futility of life.

Within the vast fabric of human existence, the quest to uncover meaning amidst apparent futility serves as evidence of the enduring strength and imaginative capacity inherent in every person. By accepting the irrationality of life, facing the uncertainty of existence with bravery, and utilizing the shared knowledge of personal stories, people can not only discover their own significance but also actively participate in the continuous process of creating human understanding. When confronted with situations that appear to lack significance, the human spirit possesses an extraordinary ability to generate meaning, thereby establishing a purposeful direction amidst the existential uncertainties that define the human condition.

Chapter 8
Rebel

"With rebellion, awareness is born."
Albert Camus

Within the immense scope of the cosmos, humans frequently encounter the seeming apathy of the universe in their pursuit of significance and direction. This chapter explores the profound idea of rebelling against a universe that appears to lack any inherent meaning. Grounded in existential philosophy, literature, and psychological viewpoints, we examine the complex dynamics of resistance in response to cosmic nihilism and the transformative function of rebellion in generating novel and improved outcomes.

Cosmic nihilism, which is the conviction in the intrinsic lack of meaning or purpose in the universe, establishes the foundation for a philosophical revolt. This viewpoint implies that, when considering the vastness of the universe, the existence of humans does not possess inherent importance. The consequences of such a perspective are significant, as it forces individuals to confront the challenge of discovering meaning in a universe that appears to be apathetic towards their endeavors.

Existential philosophy, advocated by intellectuals such as Jean-Paul Sartre and Albert Camus, presents the notion of rebellion as a reaction to the irrationality of human existence. Existential rebellion entails the refusal to passively accept and instead asserting one's own agency when confronted with an indifferent universe. This philosophical perspective promotes individuals to directly confront the concept of emptiness and actively generate significance as a form of rebellion against cosmic nihilism.

Camus' concept of absurdity captures the inherent conflict between the human longing for purpose and the apparent lack of meaning in the universe. The absurd emerges when individuals strive for a logical justification for their existence in a universe that provides none.

When confronted with this irrationality, rebellion arises as a demand for action—a rejection of inaction and a dedication to creating significance in spite of the vast emptiness of the universe.

Literature, being a reflection of the human condition, frequently acts as a deep expression of existential defiance. Literary masterpieces, such as Camus's "The Stranger" (a novel I mentioned earlier) and Sartre's "Nausea," delve into the lives of characters who defy the apathetic nature of the universe by forging their own interpretations of existence. These narratives serve as a means of expressing the profound battle against nihilism, encouraging readers to contemplate the consequences of rebellion in their personal experiences.

Psychological analyses of resistance against cosmic nihilism explore the complexities of human awareness. The pursuit of significance, inherent in the human mind, can result in existential distress when faced with the apparent lack of purpose in the cosmos. Psychologically, rebellion serves as a coping mechanism, actively addressing the existential emptiness and promoting resilience and a sense of meaning in the face of the vast cosmic void.

Existential rebellion highlights the significance of authenticity, which entails a steadfast dedication to living in alignment with one's values and beliefs. Authenticity emerges as a fundamental principle in the revolt against cosmic nihilism, as individuals traverse the existential terrain with honesty and self-consciousness. Rebellion, when based on genuineness, surpasses simple disobedience; it transforms into a deliberate decision to live in accordance with one's genuine identity.

Creativity, in its diverse manifestations, functions as a potent means of defiance against a universe that lacks inherent meaning. Engaging in artistic, scientific, and intellectual activities serves as a form of rebellion, as it defies the apathetic nature of the universe and adds to the intricate fabric of human interpretation and significance. When seen as an act of rebellion, the creative process serves as evidence of humanity's ability to give meaning and purpose in the presence of nihilistic influences.

The concept of existential rebellion occurs within the domain of freedom, where individuals have the liberty to make choices, establish their own principles, and resist the existential emptiness. Nevertheless, this liberty is not devoid of its quandaries. The accountability associated with the liberty to revolt prompts inquiries regarding the essence of the generated significance. Individuals strive to find significance as they confront the gravity of their decisions and the existential ramifications of their acts of defiance.

The act of rebelling against cosmic nihilism highlights the fact that the meaning of life is subjective. Instead of pursuing an objective purpose determined by the universe, individuals undertake a journey to find subjective meaning - a meaning that is personally meaningful and reflects their individual experiences, values, and aspirations. The revolt against cosmic nihilism transforms into an introspective quest, where individuals consciously build significances that deeply align with their essence.

The enduring impact of existential rebellion resonates within the philosophical discussion on the nature of human existence. Modern intellectuals persist in grappling with the consequences of defying cosmic nihilism, investigating pathways for constructing significance in a universe that remains apathetic towards human endeavors. This ongoing philosophical dialogue prompts individuals to contemplate the lasting significance of rebellion as a reaction to the inherent irrationality of existence.

Rebellion, in the face of cosmic nihilism, goes beyond simply rejecting meaninglessness; it serves as a catalyst for generating novel and improved outcomes. The rebellious nature plays a significant role in shaping the narrative of human existence, leading to a transformative change that surpasses simple acts of defiance.

Rebellion, when harnessed in a creative manner, has the ability to generate novel ideas, innovations, and perspectives. The innate creative power within acts of rebellion against cosmic meaninglessness drives individuals to venture into unexplored realms of cognition. It stimulates individuals to challenge established conventions, cultivating an atmosphere where innovative resolutions to long-standing issues can arise.

Different domains, such as art, science, philosophy, and social change, witness the expression of creative rebellion. Artists defy traditional beauty standards, scientists scrutinize existing hypotheses, and philosophers dismantle established frameworks. Social movements, originating from defiance of established societal norms, have historically been instrumental in driving progress and reshaping societal values.

Rebellion, in the face of cosmic nihilism, fosters a tenacious resilience that empowers individuals to endure the existential trials presented by the void. When confronted with a lack of apparent purpose, the defiant nature becomes an internal reservoir of resilience, driving individuals to confront the ambiguities of life with bravery and re-solve.

The resilience cultivated through acts of rebellion is not a passive tolerance of hardship; instead, it is an active involvement with the intricacies of existence. It enables individuals to gain knowledge from failures, adjust to evolving situations, and find significance in challenges. Thus, rebellion assumes the role of a dynamic catalyst that drives individuals towards personal development and the formation of a more resilient sense of self.

Opposing cosmic nihilism also brings forth an ethical aspect, involving a deliberate decision to engage in actions that promote the improvement of both the individual and society. The ethical ramifications of rebellion encompass not only the assertion of one's values, but also the contemplation of the wider consequences of these values on the welfare of oneself and others.

Ethical rebellion prompts individuals to contemplate the repercussions of their actions and endeavor to make a constructive influence on the world. This raises the question of how the quest for individual significance can be reconciled with a collective effort to establish a fair, empathetic, and purposeful society. Rebellion, in this context, serves as a catalyst for moral metamorphosis, exerting its influence on both personal decisions and communal frameworks.

Throughout history, the act of defying established societal norms has consistently played a pivotal role in instigating transformative shifts in society. The origins of movements promoting civil rights, gender equality, environmental sustainability, and other progressive ideals can be traced back to a revolt against oppressive structures and antiquated paradigms. These actions demonstrate how the united resistance against societal injustices can result in significant and profound changes in society.

When the rebellious nature is harnessed by a group, it has the ability to challenge established power structures, dismantle unfair systems, and promote inclusiveness. Societal uprisings spark discussions on fairness and righteousness, motivating people to challenge existing conventions and imagine a community that embodies a more empathetic and equal ideology.

At an individual level, resisting the belief that life has no meaning leads to a reinterpretation of one's personal stories. Defiance, as an action, serves as a crucial turning point in an individual's life narrative, signifying a shift from passive acquiescence to active involvement in the pursuit of significance. The narrative trajectory transitions from a worldview that is determined by cosmic apathy to a narrative that is influenced by individual volition and intentional behavior.

Redefining personal narratives entails engaging in introspection, self-discovery, and a deliberate evaluation of one's values and aspirations. Individuals, in their defiance of cosmic meaninglessness, assume the role of creators of their own narratives, crafting a rich fabric of significance that deeply aligns with their essence. The transformative nature of rebellion enhances a deep feeling of self-empowerment and control over one's personal life story.

Resistance to the belief that life is meaningless on a cosmic scale is frequently manifested through scientific and technological advancements. Throughout history, scientific revolutions have been characterized by individuals who defied prevailing paradigms, questioning established theories and methodologies. The relentless quest for knowledge, fueled by an insubordinate inquisitiveness, has resulted in revolutionary breakthroughs and transformative changes that redefine our comprehension of the universe.

Technological advancements can also arise as a means of defying the constraints imposed by the natural world. The remarkable ability of humans to think creatively and solve problems has led to the development of groundbreaking technologies that have revolutionized our lifestyles, communication methods, and interactions with the world. Within this particular framework, rebellion emerges as a potent catalyst for advancement and the ongoing development of human society.

Artistic expression, as a means of defiance, plays a pivotal role in igniting a cultural revival. Artists, poets, musicians, and creators of all kinds defy established artistic conventions, questioning the prevailing standards and expanding the limits of imaginative manifestation. Oftentimes, this leads to a cultural rebirth that goes beyond the boundaries of traditional aesthetics, giving rise to innovative art forms that embody the defiant essence of the era.

Cultural rebellions, such as avant-garde movements or subversive countercultures, enhance the variety and depth of human expression. They defy societal expectations, interrogate established norms, and stimulate innovative modes of thought. The artistic defiance against the belief that life is without purpose or value serves as a way to surpass the feeling of emptiness and allows for the expression of significance and aesthetics despite the apparent lack of meaning.

The realm of education provides a fertile environment for resisting cosmic nihilism. The pursuit of knowledge, motivated by a longing to comprehend the complexities of existence, can be regarded as a defiance against ignorance and the lack of intellectual progress. The pursuit of education, characterized by the exploration of various fields and viewpoints, serves as a personal defiance against the constraints of ignorance.

Novel pedagogical methods that foster critical thinking, ingenuity, and a comprehensive comprehension of the world serve as means for defiance. By rethinking educational frameworks and prioritizing the development of curiosity and a sense of purpose, individuals are empowered to challenge a fixed perception of their intellectual capacity. Education, in this context, serves as a catalyst for personal growth by providing individuals with the necessary skills to effectively navigate the intricacies of life.

While isolated instances of defiance contribute to individual development and narrative transformations, it is the combined effect of these individual acts of rebellion that determines the course of societies and civilizations. The cumulative impact of numerous acts of rebellion against cosmic nihilism generates a cultural mindset that esteems endurance, ingenuity, moral accountability, and a dedication to societal advancement.

The cumulative influence is apparent in movements that aim to tackle systemic problems, advance justice, and champion constructive societal transformation. The interrelation of individual acts of rebellion weaves together a fabric of common beliefs, resulting in the formation of communities that embody the ideals of empowerment, inclusivity, and a collective sense of mission.

To summarize, rebellion against cosmic nihilism has a profound impact that goes beyond simple defiance. It becomes a powerful force that shapes personal stories, drives societal advancement, and encourages innovation in different fields. When the rebellious spirit is channeled in a creative and ethical manner, it possesses the ability to generate novel and improved outcomes, leading to a transformative shift that surpasses the constraints imposed by an apparently apathetic universe.

Rebellion, whether manifested in scientific investigation, artistic creation, academic endeavors, or social advocacy, serves as evidence of the enduring and innovative capabilities of the human spirit. Rebellion has the power to not only confront the sense of emptiness in life but also actively contribute to the collaborative formation of significance and direction.

As people resist the belief that life has no meaning, they take on the role of creators of a story that surpasses the limitations of a universe governed by cause and effect. The combined influence of these defiant stories contributes to a cultural environment that esteems independence, ingenuity, perseverance, and a mutual dedication to constructing a superior and more significant world. Amidst the vast indifference of the universe, the rebel stands out as a symbol of hope, actively confronting the intricacies of existence and playing a role in the ongoing process of human interpretation and significance.

Chapter 9
How to Handle Existential Despair

"The most common form of despair is not being who you are."
Søren Kierkegaard

The prevalence of existential despair, characterized by a deep sense of meaninglessness and hopelessness, has been on the rise in our contemporary society. When facing the challenges of life, it is important to confront this feeling of hopelessness without succumbing to the usual pitfalls of overused phrases, popular self-improvement fads, and dependence on spiritual leaders.

Existential despair frequently arises from a profound feeling of detachment, whether it is from oneself, others, or the world. Analyzing the origins enables individuals to comprehend and address their distinct causes of despondency.

The impact of existential despair on mental health is significant and should not be underestimated. It presents itself through symptoms such as anxiety, depression, and a pervasive feeling of uneasiness. Acknowledging these consequences is the initial stage in developing effective strategies for dealing with them. This chapter offers a range of suggestions and tips to consider when dealing with existential despair. Consider it a jumping off point.

Numerous clichés may present themselves as convenient solutions to existential despair, but frequently fail to offer long-lasting alleviation. We should analyze these clichés and reveal their constraints and promote a more profound examination of one's emotions.

Although self-help is beneficial, it frequently oversimplifies intricate matters. We should explore the limitations of exclusively relying on self-help methodologies and advocate for a more comprehensive and self-reflective approach.

Experts offer assurances and direction, yet their methodology may not be universally applicable. Gaining insight into the appeal and possible drawbacks of depending on external influences is essential for individual development.

Dependence on gurus can result in a lack of self-reliance and self-confidence. We should always examine the disadvantages of delegating one's existential quest to external sources and advocate for ourselves to regain control and responsibility for our own lives.

Each individual's journey is distinct. We should examine various coping strategies, enabling us to develop a customized set of tools for navigating existential despair.

Isolation intensifies existential despair. We should be mindful of the importance of social connections and learn to rely on friends, family, and community for support.

In addition to quantity, the quality of connections is also important. We should examine methods to foster significant connections that enhance an our sense of purpose.

Striking a balance between realism and positivity is crucial for maintaining sustainable mental well-being. We should develop a mindset that recognizes challenges while simultaneously maintaining an optimistic perspective.

Positive thinking should not come at the cost of recognizing and acknowledging challenges. We should examine pragmatic methods to foster a resilient mindset that embraces the inevitable fluctuations of life.

Art and creativity offer distinctive channels for expressing oneself. Participating in creative endeavors can function as a therapeutic means of coping with existential despair.

Mindfulness enables individuals to cultivate a state of being fully aware and engaged in the present moment. It's important to incorporate practical strategies for practicing mindfulness techniques into everyday routines, which can help in effectively coping with existential despair.

Meditation transcends mere relaxation; it can serve as a potent instrument in confronting existential despair. Learning about and trying various meditation techniques will almost always do more good than harm.

Occasionally, the assistance of a professional is indispensable. It's critical that you be aware of the indicators that signify the need to pursue therapy or counseling in order to obtain more customized assistance.

Gaining a comprehensive understanding of various therapy options and counseling approaches will enable individuals to make well-informed choices regarding their mental health progress.

Instead of comparing oneself to societal norms, we will prioritize the significance of concentrating on personal development. We need to learn how to channel our energy towards self-improvement because it can effectively counteract existential despair.

Change is an enduring aspect of life, however, it can also serve as a cause of distress. We should always examine the unavoidable nature of change and develop a mindset that welcomes transformation as an inherent aspect of the human condition.

To effectively address existential despair, a comprehensive strategy is necessary, surpassing the use of clichés, self-help techniques, and dependence on gurus. Through comprehending the origins of despair, adopting individual coping strategies, establishing meaningful connections with others, and actively exploring philosophy and creativity, individuals can effectively navigate existential difficulties with fortitude and a sense of direction.

It is important to bear in mind that the process of conquering existential despair is distinct for every individual. The task at hand involves achieving equilibrium by recognizing the challenges of existence while nurturing a mentality that promotes personal development and significance.

Chapter 10
Laugh in the Face of Nothingness

"He who laughs at himself never runs out of things to laugh at."
Epictetus

This chapter looks at the deep connection between laughing and the mind, focusing on how comedy can be used as therapy to fight the appeal of passive nihilism. There is a big problem with mental health in modern society: passive nihilism (I've tried to make that clear for nine chapters now, but in case I didn't, there it is again). I'd like to talk about how laughing can help you deal with the feeling that life is empty. I'll also make the case that laughter builds resilience and protects you mentally and emotionally from the allure of passive nihilism.

Because passive nihilism is so common in modern culture, we need to take a close look at ways to lessen its negative effects on mental health. People all over the world laugh, so it seems like a good idea to use laughter as a therapy tool in this case.

As a psychological condition, passive nihilism is marked by a deep-seated sense of meaninglessness and an unwilling acceptance of the pointlessness of life. Lack of motivation, indifference, and a diminished sense of purpose are what set it apart. It is important to fully understand the complicated nature of passive nihilism in order to come up with effective ways to lessen its effects on mental health.

Passive nihilism is becoming more popular because of changes in society and the economy, fast technological progress, and the breakdown of traditional value systems. There is a climate that is good for existential crises to happen because people are always trying to get rich and social bonds are breaking down.

Neuroscientific studies have shown that laughing makes the brain release endorphins and dopamine, which are neurotransmitters that make you feel good. Understanding how laughter works in the brain is important for realizing that it can help people who are dealing with passive nihilism.

Laughter functions as a coping tool, enabling us to reframe challenges and adversity in a more optimistic way. Moreover, the communal aspect of laughter promotes interpersonal bonds, creating a network of assistance that strengthens one's ability to cope with existential difficulties.

Comedy and laughter are surprisingly important in philosophical traditions. Philosophers like Aristotle and Kierkegaard have thought about the link between comedy, making sense of things, and existential questions throughout history.

The way Kierkegaard thought about laughter was by dividing it into two groups: the *demonic* and the *comic*. In "Either/Or," Kierkegaard talks about the idea of *demonic* laughter as a mean way to have fun that involves rejecting and making fun of other people. As Kierkegaard says, this kind of laughter shows a shallow and morally questionable interest in the world. A person who laughs in a way that puts themselves between real human connection and empathy is showing that they are distant.

Alternatively, Kierkegaard sees the idea of the *comic* as a more moral and elevated form of entertainment. Kierkegaard said that the funny comes out when people realize how limited and pointless life is. Unlike demonic laughter, which tries to boost one's own status by putting others down, comic laughter recognizes the common human experience and shows how we all understand life's ironies and paradoxes.

The next time you are listening to a "comic," think about which type of comedy he has embraced for his routine.

This study of laughter by Kierkegaard is linked to his main philosophical work, which is his criticism of the aesthetic and ethical views on life. The evil laughter is like the aesthetic point of view, which is characterized by a selfish desire for fun and a lack of moral obligations. In contrast, the laughter in *comics* is very much in line with an ethical view of life, since it shows that people are aware of their duties to others and the moral necessity of living together and depending on each other.

In addition, Kierkegaard's ideas about laughter shed light on how he understood irony. According to Kierkegaard, irony and the funny go hand in hand and offer a deeper way of interacting with life than simple opposites. As a way to keep oneself aware, irony helps people get through the complicated parts of life without giving up on hope, which can happen when you only think about beauty or pleasure.

Kierkegaard's view on laughter makes us think about the moral aspects of comedy and how it can help us build real relationships with other people. By making a distinction between the *demonic* and the *comic*, Kierkegaard gets people to think about what they're laughing at and how it affects their relationships with others. By doing this, he encourages people to think more deeply about the moral duties that come with being able to enjoy life.

It looks like laughing might be a rebellious power that can fight pessimism, which is a key idea we talked about earlier. Thoughts of laughing in the face of the abyss might be just what someone needs to get through the worst times of their life.

Chapter 11
A Stoic Approach

"The happiness of your life depends upon the quality of your thoughts."
Marcus Aurelius

When nihilism and stoicism come together, they create a philosophical space where the lack of a purpose meets the strength of moral excellence. Within this chapter, the ideas of stoicism are explored and shown to be very useful for people who are dealing with negative ideas. I'd like to look into the basic ideas of stoicism and see how they can be used to deal with the void of nihilism. Also, I'd like to make it clear how developing a stoic mindset can help people who are facing existential problems find meaning and direction.

As we move through the complicated landscape where stoicism and nihilism meet, we come to a place where existential questions and moral strength also meet. I will look at how these different philosophies can work together in this chapter, showing how stoicism can be a powerful way to deal with the void that lack of purpose leaves.

The school of thought called stoicism, which has roots in ancient Greece, has stood the test of time. It will always be useful because it stresses developing virtue as a way to deal with life's problems. According to the stoic philosophy, people should live in harmony with nature. This idea includes not only the natural world, but also the natural logic that guides human behavior.

When faced with the overwhelming nihilistic abyss, the stoic virtues of wisdom, courage, temperance, and justice can help people build a strong fortress. Stoicism is based on the idea of wisdom, which tells people to learn more about the world and their place in it. When life seems pointless, the search for wisdom becomes a lighthouse that helps one find their way through the maze of life.

When you are up against nihilism, courage, which is another cardinal virtue, becomes very important. The stoic sage is not indifferent; instead, he faces the void with courage because he knows that facing the harsh realities of life takes strength and courage. This is a call to face the abyss with unwavering resolve, recognizing the difficulties without giving up.

When a stoic fights nihilism, temperance, which is the virtue of self-discipline, is very useful. People can keep their inner selves in check by practicing moderation in a world full of things that can be super overwhelming. Stoics train their minds to be disciplined so they can find purpose and meaning within themselves by resisting the pull of nihilistic despair.

Justice, the last stoic virtue, goes beyond individual concerns and includes a sense of duty to all people, as they are all connected. People who are struggling with nihilistic views find that the search for justice changes them. It makes them want to make the world a better place, even if they don't feel like they have a purpose in life. This creates a sense of community and well-being.

The dichotomy of control, or the difference between what we can control and what we can't, is one of the most important ideas in stoicism. When facing the nihilistic void, this contrast becomes even more important. The stoic way of thinking says that people should work on developing their inner virtues instead of worrying about what other people do, since we can't always change their actions.

When people think about nihilism, they might feel helpless and overwhelmed by the vastness of a universe with no purpose. By turning our attention inward, stoicism gives us a useful way to deal with this existential crisis. Focusing on internal virtues and personal growth gives people back control in a world that might otherwise seem uninterested in their problems.

People can free themselves from the chains of external factors by changing the way they think about themselves. Nihilism says that the universe doesn't have any meaning on its own, but stoicism says that people can find meaning in the very act of improving themselves. Knowing that outside factors can make life difficult, the stoic sage focuses on developing a good character, which helps them create a meaningful life on a personal level.

The idea of amor fati, or loving one's fate, comes from stoicism. When the world doesn't seem to have any purpose, accepting your fate becomes a very important thing to do. The stoic, who is strong, faces existential problems with a sense of purpose that comes from within. They create meaning in the process of navigating life's uncertainties.

Nihilism says that life is just a bunch of random events that don't have any meaning. Amor Fati disagrees with this view. For instead, it encourages people to see their experiences, good and bad, as important parts of their own story. Your life story is always being written, and every victory and defeat adds to it. Amor Fati tells people to welcome this story with open arms.

Stoicism says that accepting your fate means completely giving up on the present moment. It's a recognition that every moment has value on its own, even when things seem chaotic and pointless. This kind of acceptance makes you stronger when things go wrong, turning problems into chances to learn more about yourself and grow.

When people use stoic ideas to deal with the nihilistic void, they start a journey of self-discovery that changes them. The stoic philosophy becomes a guiding light, giving meaning and direction to the parts of life that seem random and pointless. Being a stoic means more to them than getting approval from other people. They find meaning in striving for moral excellence and character improvement.

Stoicism disagrees with the idea that meaning comes from outside sources and is just waiting to be found. Instead, it says that meaning is something that each person creates on their own by consciously working on their virtues and navigating the challenges of life. The stoic forge is a figure of speech for a workshop where people make their own sense of purpose by using the raw materials of their experiences to hammer out meaning.

The process of making meaning requires people to interact with the world on purpose. Stoics think that virtue should be sought as an end in itself, not as a way to get to another goal. People find happiness in the pursuit of moral excellence, even when their outside circumstances might make them feel like they have no purpose in life. People can change their lives in the stoic forge, where they are involved in making their own future. This goes beyond the nihilistic view that life has no meaning on its own.

As this exploration comes to a close, it's clear that the meeting of nihilism and stoicism doesn't lead to a dead end. Instead, it creates a way for people to face the void with unwavering strength. Stoicism's timeless wisdom helps us find our way through the philosophical landscape where moral strength meets lack of purpose. There is hope in the stoic way of thinking when people are facing existential problems. It tells people to find their own meaning in the vastness of the nihilistic universe.

Stoicism as a philosophy is more than just a set of ideas; it's also a way of life for people who don't feel like they have a purpose in life. The stoic way of life shines brightly in the darkness of nihilism, showing the way to personal growth, strength, and making meaning. When people combine these philosophies, they get not only a philosophical base, but also a strong mindset that helps them get through life's challenges with purpose and virtue.

When people reject nihilism and embrace stoicism instead, they start a life-changing journey where they learn that not having an outside purpose does not mean that their life has no purpose. Instead, stoicism tells them to build their own meaning, making a sense of significance that can stand up to the existential problems that the void brings up. The stoic beacon keeps shining, calling people to embrace the virtues, find their way through the duality of control, and find meaning in their own life's fire.

Chapter 12

Hygge

"Happiness consists more in small conveniences or pleasures that occur every day, than in great pieces of good fortune that happen but seldom to a man in the course of his life."

Benjamin Franklin

Our world is full of existential doubts and feelings of nihilistic detachment. However, the Danish concept of "hygge" offers a compelling way to help us deal with the difficulties of modern life. Hygge, which means a feeling of warm comfort and happiness in general, has become famous around the world for its ability to counteract the emptiness that nihilistic views cause. This chapter looks at where hygge came from and what it means at its core. It also looks at how its principles can help people find meaning, connection, and direction in a world where existential nihilism is common.

Hygge, pronounced "hoo-ga," is a Danish term that goes beyond a basic dictionary definition. The term refers to a cultural and lifestyle concept that revolves around creating a welcoming and comfortable environment that promotes a feeling of contentment, wellness, and sociability. Hygge encompasses more than just physical environments and is essentially about embracing moments of satisfaction, connection, and simplicity.

Hygge comes from Denmark in the 18th century and is closely linked to the country's social and communal norms. Hygge was first associated with the countryside in Denmark. It has since grown into a way of thinking about how to handle different parts of life and a complete approach to overall well-being.

Using a nihilistic point of view, where normal sources of meaning are questioned or thrown out, hygge provides a way to make deep connections. By consciously focusing on interpersonal relationships and creating shared experiences, people can effectively fight the isolating effects of nihilism and find their own worth in the comforting embrace of human connection.

Hygge encourages mindfulness, which lets people fully enjoy and appreciate life's simple pleasures. In a world that sometimes seems pointless, hygge helps people become more mindful and find meaning in the things they do in the present, like enjoying a warm cup of tea, having deeply meaningful conversations, or taking in the beauty of nature.

Nihilism makes people feel restless and like life has no point. Hygge, on the other hand, focuses on comfort and coziness. Making comfortable spaces, like with soft blankets, soft lighting, or calming scents, can help you feel better when you're in the existential abyss. Hygge makes places feel cozy, which is a nice change from the cold apathy that is often associated with nihilism.

Hygge puts an emphasis on simplicity as a basic principle. When people are having existential doubts, the constant pursuit of extravagance and material possessions may seem pointless. Adopting a minimalist lifestyle, on the other hand, helps people find happiness in the simple and basic things in life. Hygge says that the real value of simplicity lies in its ability to find meaning in the simple things we do.

Hygge is based on the idea that people should work together and get to know each other. Creating a sense of community is a deep and meaningful response in a nihilistic setting where individualism can make people feel even more alone. The idea behind hygge is that people are happier when they are with other people, whether they are eating, gathering, or doing activities together.

Hygge encourages careful and thoughtful consumption, which calls into question the kind of excessive consumerism that nihilistic views often criticize. By making conscious choices about things like food, decor, and lifestyle, people can find happiness and meaning by focusing on excellence instead of abundance. This idea fits with the idea that real happiness comes from interacting with the world in a planned and purposeful way.

Getting involved with nature is another important part of hygge. It is possible for nihilism to make people lose touch with nature. Hygge encourages people to find comfort and motivation in nature. Nature can help you feel better and bring people together, whether you're taking a walk in the park, hiking in the mountains, or just noticing how the seasons change.

A central part of hygge is the ritual of candlelight. The soft light that candles give off creates an atmosphere of coziness and closeness that goes beyond physical comfort to bring about emotional and spiritual peace. By lighting candles, you can symbolically fight the darkness of your own life and make a space feel cozy.

One important part of hygge is eating with other people. Whether it's a meal with family, a get-together with friends, or a moment to indulge in delicious food by yourself, enjoying it becomes a joyful celebration of life's little pleasures. The idea of hygge encourages people to enjoy tastes, appreciate the skill of cooking, and find happiness in eating with others.

The practice of making reading spaces that are comfortable and getting lost in books is a form of hygge that goes along with the search for meaning and purpose. Literature gives people the chance to look at a lot of different points of view, do in-depth philosophical research, and find comfort in stories that really connect with their own existential thoughts. The act of reading turns into a hygge ritual that can be used as both a way to escape reality and acquire new knowledge.

The addition of hygge to daily activities turns simple tasks into important rituals. The Danish concept of hygge tells people to plan their days and make time for moments of comfort and well-being, like taking a relaxing bath in the evening or enjoying a cup of coffee in the morning.

Hygge encourages accepting flaws, which is important for fighting the need to be perfect, which can be made worse by nihilistic worries. The atmosphere in hygge spaces is warm and welcoming, accepting of flaws and valuing the real essence of the present moment. In the midst of life's uncertainties, this atmosphere helps you feel kind to yourself.

As a way to fight the feeling of emptiness in life, hygge encourages people to become more grateful and mindful. People can shift their focus from what they might be missing to what they already have by noticing and appreciating the simple pleasures in life. When you're having existential doubts, expressing gratitude can be a powerful way to keep a positive attitude and keep your sense of satisfaction alive.

Hygge is a way to relax in a world where people are too focused on themselves. The communal parts of hygge can help people who are struggling with the existential philosophy of nihilism, which is often linked with feelings of being alone and detached. Focusing on shared experiences, mutual pleasure, and how people in a community depend on each other is the opposite of nihilism's tendency to make people feel alone.

Even though the Danish culture is where hygge comes from, its ideas are not limited to that place. Because people's lives are so different, hygge practices can be used in a wide range of cultural settings. While people all over the world struggle with the problems that nihilistic views cause, the principles of hygge offer a way for everyone to find meaning, comfort, and community.

With hygge becoming more popular, there is a chance that it will be used for commercial purposes. Hygge may lose some of its authenticity as lifestyle trends and goods with hygge themes become popular. It may become a marketable item instead of a real cultural and philosophical tradition. Because hygge is becoming more popular, some people worry that adopting it just to be trendy might not be as good for your health as it really is.

As some critics say, the ideas behind hygge might unintentionally hide or avoid the harsh realities of nihilism, even though they claim to bring comfort and bring people together. People may be accused of escaping the problems that come with a life that doesn't have any meaning by creating comfortable environments and focusing on enjoyable interactions.

There are people who say that hygge's traditions and customs can still be based on individualism, even though the concept values community and unity. Even if close and comfortable spaces are created and personal well-being is emphasized, the structural problems that lead to nihilistic views might not be completely fixed. Some people say that we need to look at the causes of nihilism from a bigger, more sociopolitical perspective in order to deal with them as a group.

Hygge is a dynamic philosophy that goes beyond cultural boundaries because it can be used in different situations. While some people are having a hard time with nihilism's complicated ideas, hygge provides a simple and easy-to-understand framework for creating a sense of purpose and community. Putting an emphasis on simplicity, unity, and mindfulness gives people useful ways to deal with the existential problems of modern life.

To get the most out of hygge as a response to nihilism, people need to really follow its rules. People who are interested in hygge shouldn't give in to shallow trends. Instead, they should try to build real relationships, learn to appreciate others, and accept their flaws as part of being human. When you approach hygge with sincerity, it turns into a deep philosophy that goes beyond just nice lifestyle choices.

As people try to understand nihilism and find meaning in a world that doesn't seem to care, the study of hygge and the ideas that support it leads to more conversation. People can use hygge in a way that makes them stronger, brings people together, and gives them a sense of direction by learning about its cultural roots, rituals, and core beliefs. This is a powerful way to deal with the problems that nihilism causes.

In conclusion, the idea of hygge is a deep and interesting philosophical alternative to nihilism. By following the ideas of comfort, connection, and mindfulness, people can build strong defenses against the existential emptiness that nihilistic views cause. Hygge is a complete way to improve your health and happiness, giving you a sense of purpose and happiness even when life is uncertain.

Chapter 13
Examine Your Life

Within the realm of philosophical contemplation on human existence, the directive to "examine life" reverberates throughout history, echoing the sagacity conveyed by the ancient Greek philosopher Socrates. This chapter explores the deep importance of avoiding a passive lifestyle and the necessity of regularly evaluating one's life. By incorporating Socratic philosophy, psychological insights, and contemporary perspectives, this work examines how active reflection can be a powerful tool for navigating the intricate aspects of existence.

Socrates, a prominent figure in Western philosophy, advocated for the Socratic method—a dialectical approach focused on questioning, dialogue, and self-reflection. The elenchus, a method of inquiry that reveals contradictions and encourages self-reflection, is the fundamental basis of Socratic wisdom. This approach surpasses mere intellectual investigation; it is an opportunity to actively involve oneself in the fundamental inquiries of existence.

Socrates' teachings center around the assertion that a life that is not subjected to examination is devoid of value (i.e. *not worth living*). This statement emphasizes the inherent importance of introspection in shaping a purposeful and meaningful life. Socrates argues that failing to consciously examine one's beliefs, values, and actions condemns a person to a passive life lacking genuine comprehension and satisfaction.

Passive existence, characterized by an avoidance of self-reflection and an acceptance of the status quo (not to be confused as the antithesis of hygge), often masquerades as comfort. Yet, hidden beneath the appearance of comfort and calmness, there is a risk of becoming stagnant and experiencing a gradual loss of individual control. The deceptive appearance of a comfortable, unquestioned existence conceals the capacity for personal development, self-exploration, and the quest for a deeper comprehension of one's own being.

Existential philosophers like Jean-Paul Sartre and Albert Camus examine the dangers of living a passive life in response to the inherent absurdity of existence. Sartre's concept of "bad faith" emphasizes the inclination to avoid accountability by adhering to societal norms, whereas Camus' notion of the absurd emphasizes the necessity of actively rebelling against a world that lacks inherent significance. Both viewpoints highlight the crucial importance of engaging in thoughtful introspection when facing the existential emptiness.

Engaging in active reflection acts as a catalyst for enhancing personal agency and empowerment. Through a purposeful analysis of their beliefs, choices, and values, individuals actively influence the direction of their lives. Reflection serves as a means to align one's actions with their true self, promoting a sense of independence and direction.

Active reflection naturally leads to self-discovery. The process reveals various strata of personal identity, shedding light on concealed aspects of one's character, ambitions, and capacity. When viewed through a Socratic perspective, self-discovery is essentially the same as self-realization. It involves continuously uncovering truths, questioning assumptions, and embracing the ever-changing nature of personal development.

Modern psychological and spiritual practices emphasize the significance of mindfulness and contemplation in promoting well-being. Mindfulness, derived from practices like Buddhism, promotes the development of conscious awareness of the present moment. Contemplative practices, such as meditation and reflective journaling, offer opportunities for deliberate introspection and contribute to improved cognitive clarity, emotional adaptability, and a more profound sense of inner self-awareness.

Narrative psychology asserts that individuals form their identities by means of storytelling. Active reflection entails the deliberate and ongoing process of constructing and modifying the personal story that encompasses one's life experiences. Through deliberate introspection of life experiences, obstacles, and successes, individuals construct a cohesive and purposeful narrative of their own identity. The narrative identity, in return, impacts perceptions, motivations, and potential future outcomes.

Maintaining a reflective journal is an effective method for engaging in active reflection. Writing enables a systematic examination of thoughts, emotions, and experiences. Journaling reveals internal conversations, enabling individuals to track recurring themes, recognize areas for personal development, and record the changing story of their lives.

Embracing the essence of Socratic dialogue entails actively participating in introspective or interactive discussions. This dialectical discourse stimulates a more profound scrutiny of beliefs and values through the exchange of ideas, perspectives, and questions. Dialogue is a dynamic tool that promotes active reflection, intellectual curiosity, and mutual understanding.

Incorporating reflective rituals into one's daily routine cultivates a practice of deliberate introspection. Whether engaged in morning reflections, evening evaluations, or occasional self-examination retreats, these rituals establish specific environments for deep self-reflection. By incorporating regular self-reflection into their routine, individuals approach life with a heightened consciousness and a deliberate dedication to personal development.

Active reflection encompasses not only personal introspection but also incorporates external feedback and a range of diverse viewpoints. Obtaining feedback from reliable mentors, friends, or participating in communities of discussion brings in novel perspectives and confronts preconceived notions. The exchange of ideas fosters a cooperative and introspective process, enhancing one's self-awareness.

Active introspection encompasses moral aspects, especially when it comes to the domain of making choices. The significance of Socrates' focus on moral introspection lies in the value of ethical self-examination. Through deliberate contemplation of the ethical ramifications of their decisions, individuals foster a profound sense of moral obligation and make a valuable contribution to the overall ethical framework of society.

In addition to personal introspection, Socratic wisdom also encompasses the realm of society. Active reflection encompasses the process of contemplating one's position within the community, comprehending the intricacies of social interactions, and actively participating in discussions related to civic matters. It is morally necessary to explore life, which includes the duty to actively contribute to the overall welfare of society.

Ultimately, the call to thoroughly scrutinize existence, as championed by Socrates, arises as a profound and multifaceted endeavor. The chapter has examined the importance of avoiding a passive lifestyle and the lasting worth of self-reflection, covering philosophical principles and modern viewpoints. Active reflection transforms into a dynamic conversation that continuously explores the intricacies of existence, promotes personal development, and enhances the moral framework of both the individual and society.

As individuals engage in active introspection, they embrace the Socratic principle, recognizing that self-analysis is not a fixed endpoint but a continuous endeavor. An introspective and resilient life, when thoroughly explored, serves as evidence of humanity's ability to seek wisdom amidst life's intricate challenges.

Chapter 14
Choose Tea

"The sea has neither meaning nor pity."
Anton Chekhov

Anton Chekhov, a renowned author proficient in crafting concise narratives and astutely perceiving the intricacies of human nature, encapsulated the multifaceted nature of life with a single, poignant statement: "What a fine weather today! Can't choose whether to drink tea or to hang myself." This seemingly contradictory phrase captures the dual nature of human existence—the simultaneous acknowledgement of the splendor of life and the underlying presence of existential anguish. This chapter examines the various aspects of Chekhov's quote, investigating its significance in comprehending the complex interaction between ordinary and profound elements, as well as the contrasting emotions of joy and melancholy, within the fabric of human life.

Anton Chekhov, a prominent Russian dramatist and author of short stories, is widely recognized for his profound examination of existential themes. His works frequently explore the complexities of human relationships, the vulnerability of life, and the elusive essence of happiness. The quote in question encapsulates Chekhov's nuanced viewpoint, which simultaneously acknowledges the joys of life while recognizing the pervasive undercurrent of existential inquiry.

Chekhov's reflection on weather, tea, and the possibility of self-inflicted harm reverberates throughout the wider Russian literary tradition, characterized by a tendency towards introspection and melancholy. Russian literature, ranging from the works of Dostoevsky to Tolstoy, has explored the intricate depths of the human mind, often treading the delicate boundary between exquisite beauty and existential anguish.

Chekhov's remark about the pleasant weather provides a paradoxical backdrop for examining the contradictory essence of existence. The pleasant weather, commonly linked to happiness, energy, and the pure enjoyment of admiring the beauty of nature, serves as the setting in which the existential dilemma takes place. The contrast between pleasant weather and the consideration of suicide generates a sense of unease that encapsulates the conflicting aspects of the human condition.

Chekhov skillfully captures the contrast between the ordinary and the profound by presenting the options of drinking tea or contemplating self-harm. Engaging in the act of consuming tea, a habitual practice, represents the regular and soothing elements of everyday existence. However, reflecting on suicide delves into the profound despair of existence, uncovering the hidden current of deep inquiry that exists alongside the ordinary routines of daily life.

Chekhov's quote suggests that existential despair is not depicted as a singular occurrence, but rather as a constant presence intertwined with the essence of life. It extends beyond moments of crisis or personal tragedy and exists alongside the ordinary, the mundane—a presence that even affects pleasant weather and the simple act of enjoying a cup of tea.

Chekhov's examination of existential anguish reverberates as a manifestation of the collective human condition. The acknowledgment that despair can permeate even the most ordinary moments highlights the all-encompassing quality of existential questioning. The universality of this invites readers to confront the intricacies of their own emotional landscapes, recognizing the possibility of joy and despair coexisting in the everyday fabric of life.

Chekhov's quote portrays the act of drinking tea as a ritualistic and comforting activity, symbolizing the search for solace and normality amidst existential uncertainty. Incorporating tea into the contemplation of despair introduces additional layers of symbolism, as tea frequently symbolizes a break, a moment of reflection, and a communal cultural tradition that promotes bonding and comfort.

The juxtaposition of the comforting ritual of tea drinking with the contemplation of self-harm creates a paradox that amplifies the complexity of human emotions. The act of seeking comfort and establishing a routine becomes intertwined with deep existential contemplation, emphasizing the complex interaction between the mundane and the extraordinary in shaping our emotional experiences.

Chekhov's quote corresponds to the existentialist themes that became prominent during the 20th century. Existentialism, a philosophical movement, confronts the fundamental absurdity of human existence, which arises from the conflict between the pursuit of meaning and the acknowledgment of life's inherent absence of objective purpose. Chekhov's reflection embodies an existentialist perspective, recognizing the inherent absurdity intertwined in the essence of ordinary existence.

Chekhov's quote encourages us to embrace the intricacy of human emotion. This challenges the oversimplified narratives that classify emotional experiences into dichotomous extremes—such as happiness or sadness, joy or despair. The quote's expression of duality exemplifies the complex and sometimes contradictory essence of human emotions, encouraging a more nuanced comprehension of emotional terrains. It serves as a reminder to resist the tendency to oversimplify emotional experiences in a world that often does so. The mind is a very complicated place where different emotions can exist at the same time. By recognizing and accepting the intricate nature of their emotions, we can effectively navigate the diverse and intricate aspects of our emotional experiences without succumbing to overly simplistic explanations.

Chekhov's reflection reveals the subtle boundary that distinguishes despair from hope, a boundary that is frequently indistinct in the intricate interplay of human emotions. The decision between tea and suicide signifies a critical juncture where individuals hover on the brink of this delicate boundary, wrestling with the contrast between life's possible pleasures and its inherent difficulties.

The inherent ambiguity of the choice presented in the quote mirrors the ambiguity of existential choices. The trajectory of life is characterized by unpredictability, and the coexistence of seemingly insignificant decisions and deep existential contemplation encapsulates the core of navigating this ambiguity. The act of making a choice, whether it is to adopt the habit of drinking tea or to confront the profound sense of meaninglessness, serves as a manifestation of the human ability to exercise control and make decisions in the face of the unpredictable nature of life.

Chekhov demonstrates literature's exceptional ability to express the complicated nature of human emotion. Literature functions as a reflective medium that portrays the complex interplay between happiness and sadness, encouraging readers to delve into the intricate and diverse aspects of their own emotions. Literature provides individuals with profound insights into the complexities of the human condition, surpassing superficial representations. This fosters empathy and facilitates a more profound comprehension of the collective challenges and successes that shape our identity.

The investigation of Chekhov's quote reveals a convergence between literature and philosophy. The narrative of the text explores existential themes that evoke philosophical contemplations regarding the essence of life, the fundamental nature of existence, and the inherent human quest for meaning. This convergence emphasizes the mutually beneficial relationship between literature and philosophy in clarifying the intricacies of the human experience.

Chekhov's quote underscores the significance of recognizing the full range of one's emotions, thereby impacting mental health and overall well-being. The acknowledgement that feelings of despair can coexist with the enjoyment of pleasant weather underscores the significance of embracing a wide range of emotions. Through the recognition and embrace of a comprehensive spectrum of emotions, individuals can cultivate resilience and cultivate more effective strategies for managing difficulties.

Chekhov's contemplation acts as a catalyst for destigmatization in a society that frequently stigmatizes discussions about despair and mental health challenges. The recognition that existential despair can arise even in moments of apparent normality defies societal taboos regarding mental health. Destigmatization entails facilitating candid discussions regarding the intricacies of emotional encounters, fostering empathy, and advocating for mental health awareness.

Chekhov's quote is in accordance with the principles of existential philosophy, specifically acknowledging despair as an inherent element of human existence. Existentialism, which focuses on individual accountability, liberty, and the confrontation of life's inherent irrationalities, offers a structure for comprehending the intricacies encompassed in Chekhov's reflection.

The philosophical notion of absurdity, as examined by thinkers such as Albert Camus, finds a parallel in Chekhov's depiction of pleasant weather and the contemplation of ending one's own life. The experience of absurdity arises from the conflict between the human longing for purpose and the perceived lack of meaning in the universe. This becomes evident in the everyday decisions that individuals encounter, emphasizing the inherent contradictions of existence.

Chekhov's contemplation prompts readers to ponder the significance of life, not through extravagant stories, but within the framework of ordinary decisions. The act of selecting between tea and despair serves as a microcosm of existential inquiry, representing a moment when individuals wrestle with the profound significance inherent in the mundane. This invitation to reflect corresponds with existential philosophy's emphasis on the individual's obligation to establish significance in a seemingly apathetic universe.

Instead of giving in to a sense of meaninglessness and hopelessness when confronted with the inherent irrationalities of life, Chekhov's reflection serves as an encouragement to accept and welcome the absurdity. Embracing absurdity entails acknowledging the absence of inherent significance and deriving freedom from the process of constructing individual significance. Within the conflict between tea and despair, individuals can find the power to infuse their lives with personal meaning.

To summarize, Chekhov's quote captures the complex and varied aspects of the human experience, encouraging readers to explore the vast landscape of happiness, sadness, and contemplation of existence. The pleasant weather serves as a symbol for the fleeting moments of beauty in life, while the reflection on suicide symbolizes the profound depths of existential anguish. This reflection surpasses its literary origins to reverberate as a universal investigation of the intricacies inherent in human existence.

Chekhov's contemplation prompts a demand for subtle comprehension—an acknowledgement that the significance of life is not a solitary, unchanging entity but a fluid and developing concept influenced by personal decisions and introspection. Through engaging in introspective contemplation of the contradictions inherent in existence, individuals can develop a heightened consciousness of their own emotional terrain and actively contribute to fostering a society characterized by compassion and empathy.

Chekhov's quote resonates within the realm of existential inquiry, serving as a reminder of the lasting significance of philosophical exploration in confronting life's profound inquiries. Existential philosophy, characterized by its focus on individual accountability, autonomy, and the confrontation of the irrational, offers individuals a structure to navigate the intricacies of existence and create their own trajectories in the search for significance.

When considering good weather and deciding between tea and despair, readers are reminded that the process of exploring oneself and finding meaning is inherently contradictory. It is a journey characterized by both great beauty and deep sadness. Chekhov's quote, akin to a philosophical enigma, challenges individuals to decipher the intricacies of their own being, encouraging them to fully embrace the richness of life despite the uncertainties that come with existential contemplation.

Chapter 15
Choose Coffee

"The thought of suicide is a great consolation: by means of it one gets
through many a dark night."
Friedrich Nietzsche

Within the fabric of human existence, interlaced with strands of happiness and sadness, achievements and challenges, the central motif of embracing life emerges as a steadfast storyline. The intricacies of the human condition compel individuals to navigate a landscape characterized by unpredictability, existential inquiries, and the constantly changing nuances of experience. This chapter examines the concept of choosing life, exploring the philosophical, psychological, and existential aspects that underlie this profound journey.

Existentialism is a philosophical framework that centers around individual choice, responsibility, and the creation of meaning when it comes to the question of choosing life. Existential philosophers like Jean-Paul Sartre and Albert Camus argue that the fundamental absence of meaning in life requires individuals to deliberately select their own course of action. The necessity to select existence becomes a reaction to the absence of meaning, a declaration of control in the presence of uncertainties about existence.

Albert Camus examines the conflict between humanity's longing for purpose and the apparent lack of purpose in the universe in his investigation of the absurd. Opting for existence, within the context of the absurd, becomes an act of defiance—a recognition of the fundamental irrationality of being and a dedication to constructing individual significance. The intricacies of the human experience, encompassing both moments of joy and sorrow, are embraced within the existential fabric of life.

Psychologically, the decision to fully accept and engage with life is closely connected to resilience, which is the ability to recover quickly from difficult situations and to draw strength from facing and overcoming challenges. Resilience, as a psychological concept, emphasizes the inherent capacity of humans to adjust, develop, and prosper in spite of the intricacies of life. Opting for life becomes a declaration of the unconquerable human essence, steadfast in its quest for purpose and welfare.

Cognitive and behavioral coping mechanisms are essential factors in the decision-making process regarding one's life. Individuals utilize a range of strategies, such as seeking social support and cultivating positive thought patterns, to effectively navigate the challenges and fluctuations of life. Resilience, which is the capacity to consistently choose life despite the ups and downs of existence, is enhanced by the ability to adapt and employ effective coping strategies.

Recognizing the intricacies involved in selecting life requires a direct encounter with despair, which is an inherent element of the human condition. Existential despair, as elucidated by philosophers such as Søren Kierkegaard, assumes a central role in the existential paradox. Opting for life, within this particular framework, entails facing despair not as a pathological condition but as an inherent aspect of existence. It is an acknowledgment that, even in the depths of despair, there exists the possibility for profound personal development.

Frankl's logotherapy asserts that the pursuit of meaning is a fundamental driving force in human existence. Opting for life, especially during times of hopelessness, entails actively participating in processes that create meaning. Individuals establish significance that surpasses immediate obstacles by means of relationships, creative endeavors, or existential contemplation, thereby establishing a purposeful basis for the decision to embrace life.

Humans are inherently gregarious beings, and the significance of relationships in the decision to embrace life is crucial. Social connections function as stabilizing forces, offering assistance, camaraderie, and a feeling of inclusion. The mutual exchange of actions and emotions, involving both giving and receiving, serves as a driving force for embracing life within the complex web of human interconnectedness.

Communities, regardless of whether they are based on family, culture, or society, play a role in the collective process of creating meaning. Shared values, rituals, and narratives provide a structure that helps individuals navigate the intricacies of life. The decision to adopt a positive outlook on life is magnified when considering the collective understanding and interpretation of experiences, which nurtures a sense of direction and enhances the overall strength and adaptability of the community.

In closing, the concept of selecting existence amidst the extensive intricacies of the human experience arises as a dynamic and multifaceted procedure. The narrative of choosing life is shaped by the interplay of philosophical foundations, psychological resilience, existential confrontations with despair, and the significance of relationships. Embracing life is a continuous process characterized by actively asserting one's control, developing the ability to bounce back from challenges, and finding significance in the constantly evolving nature of human existence.

The inherent complexities of making the decision to live do not diminish the difficulties; instead, they encourage individuals to actively participate in an ongoing conversation with the depth and diversity of human existence. In this conversation, the act of selecting life is portrayed as not just a single occurrence, but rather a sequence of deliberate and ongoing affirmations. It highlights the deep recognition that, despite the intricacies involved, the human spirit has the ability to rise above challenges, adjust, and ultimately opt for life.

As I've argued throughout this book, the pull towards nihilism has become a major problem in modern society, causing a sense of pessimism and uncertainty.

Nihilism is fundamentally defined by the refusal or skepticism towards the existence of inherent significance or worth in life. In a time when conventional belief systems and overarching narratives are frequently deconstructed or challenged, we are faced with the existential emptiness that remains after such dismantling. Residing in a world that appears to be on the verge of lacking significance can be confusing, but it is precisely in this void that we must strive to find an individual and genuine purpose.

An essential element in dealing with nihilism is developing an elevated level of self-awareness, something I'm constantly pushing across every book I've written and every video I've posted. Amidst a seemingly purposeless world, the introspective journey becomes an essential guide, perhaps our only guide. Participating in activities such as mindfulness, self-reflection, and contemplative exercises allows us to investigate the intricacies of our own consciousness. During this process, we can discover hidden passions, values, and aspirations that can act as guiding lights in the seemingly directionless vastness.

In addition, and as I've mentioned throughout this book, existential philosophers like Jean-Paul Sartre and Albert Camus provide deep

understanding of the human condition within a nihilistic framework. Sartre's notion of existential freedom underscores the obligation that accompanies the lack of predetermined significance. By embracing this liberty, or *freedom* as he argued it, we have the ability to shape our own destiny, constructing a unique personal story despite the indifferent nature of the universe.

Camus, however, presents the concept of the absurd, a personal favorite of mine if that wasn't apparent, which refers to the inherent contradiction between the human longing for purpose and the apparent lack of meaning in the universe. To fully embrace the concept of absurdity, we must recognize the inherent conflict between our natural inclination to seek purpose and the impossibility of discovering definitive solutions. Within this tension, a distinct type of significance can be created - a recognition of the irrationality of existence combined with a dedication to living genuinely.

Alongside philosophical foundations, fostering interpersonal relationships becomes an essential cornerstone in building a purposeful life amidst nihilism. Human relationships, encompassing familial, romantic, or platonic connections, serve as a medium for the creation and expression of shared significance. Our ability to feel empathy, compassion, and love as social beings adds a profound dimension to life that goes beyond personal feelings of meaninglessness. By establishing relationships with others, we construct small-scale representations of significance that endure the nihilistic forces.

Although personal relationships are important for creating meaning, active involvement in the wider community also has a crucial impact. Engaging in collective endeavors, such as activism, volunteerism, or collaborative projects, offers a profound sense of purpose that goes beyond individual pursuits. Within the collective endeavors,

we can discover a feeling of importance and influence that opposes the nihilistic influence.

Engaging in the acquisition of knowledge (i.e. learning something new every day) and fostering intellectual development represents a robust reaction to nihilism. By actively participating in literature, art, science, and philosophy, we are able to surpass the limitations imposed by their current circumstances. Seeking knowledge serves as a way to broaden our intellectual and emotional perspectives, cultivating a feeling of being linked to the extensive realm of human accomplishments and comprehension.

When faced with the prevailing belief that life is meaningless, embracing creativity becomes a powerful and influential force. Creativity, whether manifested in art, innovation, or problem-solving, serves as a way to infuse the world with personal meaning. The act of creation, whether through painting, music, or scientific discovery, serves as evidence of humanity's ability to surpass the nihilistic emptiness and mold the fabric of existence.

Moreover, the incorporation of physical well-being into the structure of a purposeful existence cannot be underestimated. To successfully navigate the nihilistic currents, one must possess a robust and well-functioning physique, or at least a level of physical health that doesn't contribute to feelings of sadness or depression. Consistent physical activity, a well-rounded diet, and adequate rest not only enhance physical health but also promote mental and emotional well-being. The interdependent connection between physical and mental well-being serves as a fundamental basis upon which one can build a meaningful and fulfilling existence.

Ultimately, residing in a world that is becoming more nihilistic requires a comprehensive strategy that integrates philosophical understanding, self-consciousness, interpersonal relationships, intellec-

tual involvement, creativity, and physical health. While exploring nihilism, I realize that the absence of overarching meaning structures is not a hindrance but an opportunity. This is an invitation to actively engage in the process of creating personal and shared significance, going beyond the pessimistic aspects and, in the process, bringing clarity and purpose to the darkness.

So, when you wake up tomorrow and the void is fighting for your mind, body, and essence, remember to make your cup of coffee and start your day anyway. By refusing to give in to it you are choosing to rebel. You are choosing to create purpose. You are choosing to potentially create memories and experiences that mean something to you. You are choosing an option that will ensure the people in your life will be happy about. You are choosing life and you won't regret it. I promise.

Note from the Author

It should go without saying that if you are having thoughts of suicide or are making plans to end your life, please reach out to a mental healthcare professional or call 988 to speak with someone today.

Exercises

Existential dread, characterized by a deep understanding of life's uncertainties and the lack of inherent purpose, presents an obstacle in the human existence. In order to navigate this complex terrain, individuals can participate in targeted activities aimed at promoting self-reflection, the creation of personal significance, and the ability to bounce back from adversity. The subsequent 10 exercises offer pragmatic strategies for managing existential dread.

1. Journaling for self-reflection

Allocate a designated period of time on a daily basis to document your thoughts and emotions in a journal.

Explore profound inquiries, ambiguities, and instances of apprehension.

Analyze the recurring patterns or themes in your reflections to acquire more profound understanding.

2. Practice of Mindfulness Meditation

Engage in the practice of mindfulness meditation to develop a heightened sense of awareness in the present moment.

Direct your attention towards your breath, sensations, and thoughts without forming any evaluative judgments.

Practicing mindfulness enables you to calmly and objectively observe existential thoughts without being overcome by them.

3. Clarification of Values

Contemplate your fundamental principles and convictions.

Determine the factors that provide significance and direction to your life.

Ensure that your daily actions are in line with your values in order to establish a sense of existential coherence.

4. Study of Existential Literature

Engage with existential literature, such as the writings of Jean-Paul Sartre or Viktor Frankl.

Contemplate the underlying ideas explored in these literary pieces and their connection to your personal existential worries.

Utilize literature as a catalyst to facilitate profound introspection and comprehension of oneself.

5. Significance of Establishing Objectives

Establish significant and attainable objectives in both the short and long term.

Goals offer a clear sense of orientation and meaning, serving as a remedy for existential nihilism.

Divide larger objectives into smaller, feasible tasks to achieve a feeling of advancement.

6. Philosophical Discourse

Participate in philosophical discourse with others, either individually or in a collective setting.

Engage in the exchange and examination of existential inquiries, viewpoints, and methods of dealing with challenges.

Conversations can offer diverse perspectives and foster a shared sense of comprehension.

7. Connect with Nature

Immerse yourself in natural surroundings to cultivate a profound sense of wonder and interconnectedness.

Contemplate the inherent patterns of life and their significance to existential concepts.

The natural world can provide comfort and a broader understanding when confronted with existential anxiety.

8. Artistic Manifestation

Participate in artistic endeavors such as writing, visual arts, or music.

Utilize creativity as a cathartic means to express existential concerns.

The act of creation inherently provides a feeling of purpose and fulfillment.

9. Utilizing the method of Socratic questioning

Employ Socratic questioning to interrogate and delve into your existential thoughts.

Employ incisive inquiries to reveal fundamental assumptions and convictions.

The use of Socratic dialogue promotes the development of critical introspection and the enhancement of one's viewpoints.

10. Daily Gratitude Ritual

Establish a daily routine where you express gratitude for small instances of happiness or connection.

Shift your attention away from existential worries and instead, acknowledge and value the favorable aspects of your life.

Nurturing gratitude serves as a powerful antidote to the burden of existential dread.

Reflection Questions

Core Tenets

What are your fundamental beliefs concerning the nature of existence, the significance of life, and the reason for our existence?

How do these beliefs correspond to or deviate from nihilistic perspectives?

Value Perception

How do you assess the significance of everyday experiences, relationships, and achievements?

Do you experience occasions where you find it difficult to perceive inherent worth in these facets of existence?

Influence on Decision-Making

How significantly does passive nihilism impact your decision-making process?

Do you often contemplate the importance of your decisions in the broader context of existence?

Emotional Reactions

What are the ways in which passive nihilism is evident in your emotional reactions to both difficulties and achievements?

Do certain circumstances provoke an intensified state of nihilistic contemplation?

Moral Engagement

How does the concept of passive nihilism intersect with your comprehension of morality and ethical principles?

Do you consider moral values to be significant constructs or subjective interpretations?

Interactions and Patterns within Relationships

How does passive nihilism affect your sense of connection and commitment in your interpersonal relationships?

Do nihilistic perspectives ever impact your attitudes towards others?

Search for Significance

Contemplate your continuous pursuit of significance and direction in life.

What is the impact of passive nihilism on this process of existential exploration?

Individual's Sense of Self and Uniqueness

Examine the relationship between passive nihilism and how you perceive your own personal identity.

How does nihilistic thinking impact your perception of self?

Addressing Difficulties

Reflect upon your approach to the difficulties and hardships that arise in life.

How does the adoption of passive nihilism influence the development of your coping mechanisms and resilience?

Impact on Creativity

Contemplate the influence of passive nihilism on your creative pursuits.

Does nihilistic thinking enhance or impede creative expression?

Definition of Legacy

Reflect upon your perspective regarding the creation of a significant and enduring influence or heritage.

How does passive nihilism impact your perception of the long-term importance of your actions?

Feeling of Satisfaction

Evaluate your overall level of satisfaction in different areas of life.

How much does passive nihilism enhance or diminish your perceived sense of fulfillment?

Knowledge Engagement

Reflect upon the impact of passive nihilism on your quest for knowledge and intellectual inquiry.

Does adopting a nihilistic mindset impact your drive to pursue knowledge and enlightenment?

Outlook on the Future

Evaluate your perspective on the future and objectives that span over a significant period of time.

How does the philosophy of passive nihilism impact your strategy for planning and envisioning your future?

Development of Significant Experiences

Engage in purposeful cultivation of significant experiences.

How do you manage the equilibrium between embracing a passive nihilistic perspective and actively crafting meaningful moments that have personal significance?

Further Reading: Exploring the Absurd, the Existential, and the Virtuous Life

Foundational Existentialism and Absurdism

1. **Albert Camus – *The Myth of Sisyphus***
   A seminal essay exploring the absurd condition and the question of suicide, culminating in the defiant conclusion that "one must imagine Sisyphus happy."

2. **Jean-Paul Sartre – *Existentialism is a Humanism***
   A concise defense of existentialism as a philosophy that emphasizes personal responsibility, choice, and the creation of meaning.

3. **Simone de Beauvoir – *The Ethics of Ambiguity***
   A rigorous philosophical reflection on freedom, morality, and how one lives authentically in an ambiguous world.

4. **Fyodor Dostoevsky – *Notes from Underground***

   A haunting narrative that explores alienation, defiance, and the complexities of human consciousness in the face of reason and absurdity.

Modern Takes on Existential Themes

1. **Viktor Frankl – *Man's Search for Meaning***

   A Holocaust survivor's profound account of finding meaning amidst unimaginable suffering—offering logotherapy as a path toward purpose.

2. **Mark Manson – *Everything Is F*cked: A Book About Hope****

   A blunt, humorous take on modern existential anxiety, emotional resilience, and the search for meaning in a chaotic age.

3. **Sarah Bakewell – *At the Existentialist Café***

   A narrative-driven history of the existentialist movement and its key figures, blending biography with philosophical clarity.

Virtue and the Moral Life

1. **Ryan Holiday – *The Obstacle Is the Way***

   A modern interpretation of Stoic philosophy, arguing that adversity is a necessary path to growth and virtue.

2. **Massimo Pigliucci – *How to Be a Stoic***

   A personal, accessible guide to applying Stoic principles in everyday life, grounded in the teachings of Epictetus.

3. **Pierre Hadot – *Philosophy as a Way of Life***

   A deep, scholarly look at how ancient philosophy—especially Stoicism and Epicureanism—was meant to be practiced as a lived experience.

Contemporary Explorations of Meaning

1. **Emily Esfahani Smith – *The Power of Meaning***

   An insightful exploration of four pillars of meaning—belonging, purpose, storytelling, and transcendence—grounded in contemporary research and narrative.

2. **Oliver Burkeman – *Four Thousand Weeks: Time Management for Mortals***

   A wise, often counterintuitive meditation on mortality, finitude, and how to live meaningfully in the time we have.

3. **David Foster Wallace – *This Is Water***

   A short but powerful commencement speech that confronts the difficulty—and necessity—of conscious awareness and moral choice in the face of routine and despair.